THE BOOK
OF
COLOSSIANS

A Study Into The Life Lessons of Paul

THE BOOK
OF
COLOSSIANS

A Study Into The Life Lessons of Paul

TAMA M. HENRY

EXTREME OVERFLOW PUBLISHING

EXTREME OVERFLOW PUBLISHING
A Brand of Extreme Overflow Enterprises, Inc.
P.O. Box 1811
Dacula, GA 30019
www.extremeoverflow.com

Copyright © 2024 Tama M. Henry. All rights reserved.

No part of this book may be reproduced or transmitted in any form or by any means electronic or mechanical photocopying, recording, or by any information storage and retrieval system without the prior written permission of the author, except for the inclusion of brief quotations in critical reviews and certain other noncommercial uses permitted by copyright law.

Other scriptures are from the King James Version of the Bible

Published by Extreme Overflow Publishing

Printed in the United States of America
Library of Congress Catalog in-Publication
Data is available for this title

For permission requests, contact the publisher.

Send feedback to info@extremeoverflow.com

ACKNOWLEDGEMENTS

Thanks to my Savior Lord Jesus Christ who has allowed me to challenge myself in completing my Masters of which this book is born out of. Glory be to God.

To my son Christopher, the mastermind behind this book coming to print and my daughter and granddaughter, Tasha and Gabrielle, who were relentless in documenting my hand written thesis, hence, this book. Despite the odds your encouragement has been fundamental for this success. The support of my late beloved husband, Rev Carl Henry, was a great great blessing and I thank God for him, rest in peace.

Special thanks to the Dean of my Alma mater, Rev Dr. Paul Duncan, in St Vincent and the Grenadines, who has been instrumental in academic advisory for my seminary endeavors and his tremendous support in the challenging years. God bless you, Sir.

PREFACE

To understand the book of Colossians is to understand the literary style of the book. Each lesson points out the lives of the Colossians Christians with regard to their way of life. It is an important aid to correctly understand and digest the message of the book and also the exegesis as the content follows. Once a person has understood the content, then they will eventually be admonished to apply God's word to their lives. Those who read this book will be fitted for the work of God and also to live as a child of God as the scripture teaches.

This is an exegetical work directly from the Greek text of the epistle. In a broader view of the historical, cultural, and theological issues that impinge on or arise from the text, this book will also share analogies from present situations so as to be able to preach and teach effectively on the epistles. In this study you can expect to:

- Grow in our knowledge of the content of the epistle and its historical, cultural, and theological backgrounds.
- Sharpen our skills of exegesis as well as historical and theological analysis.

- Increase our appreciation of the Apostle Paul and his place and thought in the development of the early church.
- Develop our ability to communicate the Christian faith, which we share with the first-century Christian Church.

TABLE OF CONTENTS

Preface ………………………………………	5
Chapter 1: Paul's Historical Background ………	9
Chapter 2: Survey of the Book of Colossians ….	17
Chapter 3: Introduction of Colossians………….	27
Chapter 4: The Person and Work ………………	39
Chapter 5: The Position of the Church …………	53
Chapter 6: The Responsibility of the Church ….	63
Chapter 7: The Responsibility to the World ……	71
Chapter 8: Conclusion …………………………	91
Chapter 9: Overall View ………………………..	101
Guide Answers …………………………………	111
Resources ………………………………………	119

CHAPTER 1

LIFE OF ST. PAUL; HIS HISTORICAL BACKGROUND

According to The Life and Epistles of Paul, written by Conybeare and Howson, Paul's parents were Pharisees and belonged to that same sect. He was educated by the great teacher, "Gamaliel" a Pharisee of the very same sect as Paul's father or parents. He was therefore a very educated and highly intelligent man.

To briefly specify the three effects that the teaching and example of Gamaliel may have produced on the mind of Paul, they would be as follows:

- Condor and honesty of judgment
- A willingness to study and make of us Greek authors.
- A keen and watchful enthusiasm for the Jewish law.

HENRY

His Early Boyhood Life And Character

We can see the characters exemplified in Paul's life as he said he was brought up in Jerusalem at the feet of "Gamaliel". He really meant that he lived at the Rabban's house, and ate at his table. Frankly, to sit at the feet of a teacher was a proverbial expression, as when Mary said to have sat at the feet of Jesus and heard his word. In this posture, the Apostle Paul of the Gentile who was born and spent his earliest days in the shelter of a home which was Hebrew, not in the name only but in the spirit, is where he spent his later boyhood days as an eager and indefatigable student. Paul was raised as an Israelite Jewish boy, nurtured in those histories of the chosen people which he was destined so often to repeat because of their rules and regulations in the synagogues regarding the messiah.

His Life as a Student

"From a child he knew the [1]Scriptures; which ultimately made him wise unto salvation through faith which is in Christ Jesus; as he says of Timothy in the second Epistle 3:15. During the time of his study he would keep the subtle proverbs of the sayings of renowned men in mind. For example, according to Conybeare, "He that

---

[1] "In the life of St. Paul, Benson thinks Paul was a young student during our Lord's ministry". (Page 53)

giveth his mind to the law of the Most High and occupied in prophecies." He will keep the sayings of the renowned men, and where subtle proverbs are, he will be there also. This was the pattern that was proposed to himself by an ardent follower of the Rabbis. Therefore no wonder Paul with such a standard before him and with such ardent temperament outran in Judaism many of his age and nation, being more exceedingly zealous of the traditions of his Fathers. Intellectually his mind was trained to logical acuteness, his memory became well stored with hard sentences of old, and he acquired the facility of quick and apt quotation of Scripture. Morally, he was a strict observer of the requirement of the law; and while he carefully conscientious lived life after the example of his ancestors, he gradually imbedded the spirit of a fervent persecuting zeal.

Early Manhood with Pressure

While Paul was passing through the busy years of his student life nursing the religious enthusiasm and growing in righteousness, others were advancing towards their manhood, not far from Jerusalem of whom Paul knew nothing but for whose cause he was destined to count that loss which now was his highest gain. Saul was growing more and more familiar with the outward observances of the law, and gaining that experience of the "spirit of bondage" which would enable him to understand himself, and teach others the blessings of the spirit of adoption". He was feeling the pressure of that yoke, which in the words of St. Peter, neither his father nor he was able to bear: Meanwhile, the struggles of his life in this period went by as described in the seventh chapter of Romans.[2]

Persecuting the Christians to Stephen's Death

Then John the Baptist appeared on the scene by the River Jordan, this brought the greatest event of the world's history which was finished on Calvary. The sacrifice for sin was offered at a time when sin appeared to be the most triumphant. It was at the crucifixion of the Messiah that St. John the Baptist received his Lord's dying words from the cross, and after the resurrection St. Thomas met Him, to have his doubts turned into faith. Then after, St. Stephen shed the first martyrdom, while praying for his murderers.

The first martyrdom has the deepest significance for us because it was this first occasion when Saul came before us in his early manhood. Then at the age of twenty-five or thirty years when our Lord's public ministry began, he completed his education and went from his home to Tarsus. When he said in the first letter to the Corinthians, in chapter nine verse one. "Have I not seen the Lord?" and when he

---

[2] Pages 51 Book The Life and Epistle of St. Paul. By Conybeare and Howson

also said in Second Corinthians chapter five verse sixteen, of having known Christ after the flesh, he came only to allude, in the first case to his vision on the road to Damascus and in the second to his carnal opinions concerning the Messiah. It was on this same road to Damascus that Paul really met and came in contact with Jesus. In other words, this was where his conversion got started. As he was knocked off his vehicle he heard the voice of Jesus his real Master, recognized it, and the voice said, "Saul, Saul, you are persecuting me," and not the Christians. This was done after he had ordered the death of St. Stephen.

Recognized Jesus On The Damascus Road

St. Paul was taken to the house of one Judas, while there Ananias came into the same house where Paul was and seemed to be under a fainting spell and proceeded to pray for and with him for three days. Then he laid hands on his head and as the vision was foretold immediately he was recognized as the messenger of God, even before a word was spoken. "Brother Saul, the Lord even Jesus, that appeared unto thee in the way as thou comest, hath sent me that thou might receive thy sight and be filled with the Holy Ghost". While Ananias spoke the scales fell from his eyes and he received his full sight forthwith. (Chapter 9: 18) Shortly after, he began his ministry by preaching and proclaiming the honor of the name Jesus to the children of Israel at Damascus. He was not disobedient to the heavenly vision.

Traveling, Hardships, And Testimony

St. Paul traveled to the wider regions far and near with the gospel. He suffered many hard times, times that include shipwreck, illness, loss of many possessions, hunger, and imprisonment. But all these did not detour him from the love of God. He was instrumental in winning many to Christ and claimed Timothy to be his son in the Lord. He wrote the Epistles including the book of Colossians. At the near end of his earthly life, he was able to give his testimony to his accusers and the faithful as follows. "I have fought a good fight, I have kept the faith. And now a crown of righteousness is laid up for me."

The life of Paul is truly an inspiration because of his steadfastness and unwavering faith in Christ Jesus. Although Paul was a murderer, he was cleaned up and called by Jesus Christ: He became the greatest missionary of his time. His life should cause us to hold on tighter to our Lord for a successful Christian life. God can use anyone for his glory after he or she is cleansed from sin.

STUDY POINTS

- What was Stephen's prayer while being stoned?

- Describe what fell off Paul's eyes.

- Give Paul's last testimony.

- Give the name of the person who prayed for Paul and his location.

- Describe Paul's encounter with Jesus on the Damascus road.

CHAPTER 2

THE EPISTLE TO THE COLOSSIANS

Colossae was termed the same as the Leodicea's, located in Asia Minor in the Lycus Valley, about one hundred miles east of Ephesus on the main east-west highway. The population was heterogeneous, i.e., native Phrygians, Greek colonists, and Jews. The city was deserted completely about A.D.700.Today is a place of ruins. In Colossians 2:1 it is called Leodiced. The Church at Colossae was not mentioned in the Book of Acts and it was not directly founded by the Apostle Paul. (See Liberty Bible Commentary on N.T. on Colossians 2:1). Probably during Paul's stay at Ephesus when "all they which dwelt in Asia heard the word of the Lord Jesus" (Acts 19: 23) see also Acts 18: 23, and chap. 19:26, Philemon, Aphia, Archippus, Epaphras, and other natives were converted and became effective witnesses in this area (Philemon 2; 13-19;23 & Colossians 1;6 – 8, 4; 12 – 13) The membership was composed, largely of Gentiles (Col.1:21-27, chap. 2:13) Its size was not indicated, it attained no prominence in history and was soon faded from view.

Authorship

The author claims to be Paul, (Col.1: 1 -23, 4: 8) and there is no evidence that anyone else used Paul's name to palm off this powerful polemic. This is one of the Prison Epistles and was written from Rome in 61 or 63, AD. Tychicus was the bearer of Colossians and Ephesians. (Col. 4: 7 – 8, Eph.6: 21 – 22)

Occasion of the Epistle

Epaphras who helped evangelize the Lycus Valley arrived with greetings and with disturbing news from Colossae, (Col. 1: 7-9, ch.4:12) After Paul departs from Ephesus, the "grievous wolves" (Act. 20: 29) as they were called, entered into the church playing and making havoc within, and leading many away from the truth. The Phrygians had a mystic tendency in their worship of Cybele and were susceptible to incipient Gnosticism which later developed into strange heresies. This threatening danger was both doctrinal and ethical. There was a false conception of theology characterized by mysticism regarding the person of Christ and the origin and nature of the universe. There was a false basis of morals characterized by ritualism and formalism. At Colossae there was a strict asceticism, attempting to purify lives by a code of strict prohibitions (Col.2: 20 – 23) and antinomianism (Col. 3: 5 – 7). Paul writes to express his interest in the

Colossians and to warn them against reverting to their old vices. He refutes false doctrine and proclaims the truth. He presents a full-length portrait of Christ as supreme and sufficient. (Col.2: 9: 10) Son of Man, (Humanity) and Son of God (Deity).

Relation of the Epistle To The Ephesians

In Ephesians, the emphasis is on the dignity of the Church, which is the body of Christ. In Colossians, the emphasis is on the Deity of Christ, who is the head of that body. In Ephesians, the Church is considered as oneness with Christ, while in Colossians, the Church is considered as completeness in Christ. Ephesians spoke of the Christian as being in Christ, while in Colossians; Christ is spoken of being in the Christian.

Concern and Love for the Colossian Church.

While St. Paul was at Rome in prison he wrote many of his Epistles. It was about the same time the Book of Philemon was written. After these books were written and prayed over he was able to get them to the various churches where the believers were. He did this by special messengers namely Tychicus and Onesimus who were faithful and fellow-servants. This is an indication and was mentioned that all corresponded with him in Rome, (Phil. 1:1), and many of the best (MSS) manuscripts were sent to Colossae, and this form is found in some of the later Greek writers.

While St. Paul was in Rome in prison, he received gifts or contributions from Philippi by one Epaphroditus who was a native of Colossae. So, although St. Paul did not know the Colossian Christians or the Church in person, they were recommended to him by his fellowship worker and brother in the Lord. It was also clearly seen that the Christians at the Colossian Church were very much in love with St. Paul according to the letter he sent to them and for all that they had heard about him, (Page 92, No: 3) (2 MSS). St. Paul valued their kindness very much and always lifted them up to God for their kindness.

The Colossians had a history angles worship of which St. Paul wrote them about which was a fact. In his writing to them, he did not respond to them for it. Instead, he, Paul counseled them and helped them to turn away from such things in a loving way that would have helped them to grow. Hess states in an article from, "Our Daily Bread Ministry" "Celebrate the Fruit" [1]. It's easy to develop a critical spirit towards people who are not growing spiritually according to our expectations. We can easily spot concerns that need correction, but we also need to take note of what is right. In St. Paul's letter to the Colossians Christians for example, he mentioned that the Gospel had taken root and was producing fruit in the lives of the believers there (Col. 1:6). He celebrated then by directing his thanks-giving towards God for their spiritual growth. They had come to know Jesus Christ and now were struggling against the false teachers, (Col. 2:6–8). He thanked the Lord for their deep and alluding love for all the saints for expressing tangible and sacrificial concern for them (Col.1:4). Paul also thanked God because the Colossian's faith and love grew out of their hope – the reality and assurance that this world is not the end (Col.1:5).

Today may present us with opportunities to observe fellow believers. We can be critical or celebrate their spiritual progress. Let's take the time to thank God for all the ways the Gospel of Jesus Christ has taken root and is producing fruit in the lives of others. The Apostle Paul was seen as one of the great father figures of this Church. He was so in love with the Colossian Church that he addressed them as his dearly beloved (in the spirit) even though he had never seen them in person. Even when St. Paul heard of their faults and disobedience on their part, he pointed out the matter and dealt with it very promptly, right away, or immediately[3].

These firm policies helped them to move on swiftly without a gap or weakness within themselves or with others, their spiritual lives in Paul's view had to be the very

---

[3] Kasper Cindy Hess states in "Our Daily Bread Ministry", article "Celebrate the fruit" Caxias Postal 4190, Curitiba / PR82501 -970, Brazil

example of the Christ. The Apostle Paul suffered very much for the Colossian Christians even though he was in bonds in prison. The view of his love and concern for the Colossian Christians is confirmed in (Col. 1:4) where his love was displayed by Epaphras. He also reminded them that they should not be fearful of evil spirits; His teachings to them were that their Heavenly Father had already delivered them from the kingdom of darkness and that they were already transplanted into the kingdom of his dear Son. Christ had victoriously ascended to heaven to share the divine might of his father who is at work in all mankind.

The Epistle to the Colossians

If Ephesians can be labeled the epistle portraying the "Church of Christ," then Colossians must surely be the "Christ of the Church." Ephesians focuses on the "Body"; Colossians focuses on the "Head". Like Ephesians, the little book of Colossians is divided neatly in half with the first portion doctrinal (1 & 2) and the second portion practical (3 & 4). Paul's purpose is to show that Christ is preeminent – first and foremost in everything – and the Christian's life should reflect that priority. When believers are rooted in Him, hidden in Him, and complete in Him, it is utterly inconsistent for them to live life without Him. Clothed in His love, with His peace ruling in their hearts, they are equipped to make Christ first in every area of life.

COLOSSIANS

This epistle became known as "Pros Kolossaeis," "To the Colossians," because of verse 1:2. Paul also wanted the book to be read in the neighboring church at Laodicea (4:16).

Friends of Paul Mentioned in his Letter to the Church at Colosse:

- Epaphras (1:7; 4:12)
- Tychicus (4:7)
- Onesimus *(4:9)*
- *Aristarchus (4:10)*
- *Mark (4:10)*
- *Jesus Justus (4:11)*
- *Demas (4:14)*
- *Luke (4:14)*
- *Nymphas (4:15)*
- *Archippus (4:17)*

Survey of Colossians

Focus: Supremecy of Christ and Submission to Christ

References:

- Paul, Apostle of Christ (1:1)
- Image of invisible God (1:15)
- The True Way (2:14)
- Bond of Christ (3:1)
- Put on Christ (3:5)
- Servant of Christ (4:7)
- Grace of Christ (4:18)

Divisions:

- Introduction
- Preeminence of Christ
- Freedom in Christ
- Position of the Believer
- Practice of the Believer

- Conclusion

Topic:

- Doctrinal: What Christ Did for us
- Practical: What Christ Does through us

Time & Location: Rome, A.D. 60-61

I believe that the Church in Colossae, at the time received that special letter from St. Paul to wake them up to the fact that if they really meant Jesus Christ they would have to show him up in their daily walk. They also would have to give heed to the true doctrine of Jesus Christ and not to hypocrisy. The Colossians were Gentiles, in other words, the Church there was a Gentile Church, and they were more exposed to the customs and habits of the Gentiles. This also made it easier for those Gentile Christians to fall back on doing the things they once left. However, they were properly grounded in the Lord Jesus Christ and had a strong feeling that to do so they would become a burden to St. Paul's ministry, although he had never visited them in person.

STUDY POINTS

- Was St. Paul the founder of the Church at Colossae? "Give scriptural Proof".

- What was the purpose of Paul's writing to the Colossians Church.?

- Paul emphasized the Deity of Christ in the Colossian Church, why?

- Where was Paul when he wrote the Epistle to the Colossian Church?

- According to the book of Colossians, who was the person acting as their Minister?

CHAPTER 3

THE BOOK OF COLOSSIANS

In Ch.1:1, Paul an Apostle: Paul referred to his apostleship because he was unknown to the Colossians. This refers to his authoritative title, signifying equality with the Twelve, because he has seen the risen Christ (1 Cor, 15:8). He refers to the deity of his office, he is clothed with authority and endued with power. In his official capacity, he is writing to combat error.

(Of Jesus Christ) Paul is our Lord's ambassador. He bore this commission did his work and sought his acceptance. Paul's life work was ordered by Christ; (by the will of God) this speaks of his divine appointment. His appointment was not by the Twelve, nor by the religious leaders, or his family, nor by himself.

This is an assertion of his divine authority, a declaration of his independence from all human authority, and he disclaims any individual merit or personal power. Timothy our brother; Timothy was not an apostle, he was a brother. This trusted companion was with Paul in Rome. As an act of courtesy, Paul includes Timothy in the salutation.

Timothy was Paul's spiritual son, (1 Tim. 1:2-18; 2 Tim.1:2; 1 Cor. 4:17).

To The Saints:

(Gr. Hagios) This speaks of their divine relationship. This means, the "holy ones" are again believers, not some ordinary special group. It also means, "separated ones" separated from God, separated by God, and separated from the world. This also means one belongs to God only. The main idea is not the excellence of character but separation to God for His purpose and for His service. (A faithful brethren) Believing brethren. This refers to their human relationship. They were full of faith, trusted, and trustworthy. They were loyal to Christ, as Paul refers to them, and there was no spiritual nobility in them. God has only one spiritual family and all are equal in His sight.

God doesn't put anyone above the other because he or she is of a different race, color, or of a higher educational aptitude, despite differences in cultural background or social status.

(In Christ) This speaks of the spiritual position of believers in union with Christ; this is a real mystical union. This is also in a Supernatural union with the Most High God. There is not only filial relation to God, or sons and daughters relation to God but also brotherly or sisterly relation to believers. This means that we are each other keepers and helpers one of another. Paul speaks of their faith, fraternity, and fellowship. Grace God's unmerited favor. Grace really gives us what we really don't deserve, while mercy withholds from us what we do deserve. Grace always precedes peace and peace. Peace with God and the peace of God. Peace speaks of the calm tranquility of the heart amidst disturbing circumstances and discouragements of various kinds. (From God) Who is the source of grace and more grace?

Thanksgiving. CH.1:3-8.

"We give thanks" Paul begins with thanksgiving, because there was always much to give God thanks for, and it was as if giving thanks was always on the tip of St. Paul's tongue. Thanks-giving proceeds intercession, while praise proceeds prayer. As Paul went about his thanks-giving act, he called God the Father of our Lord Jesus Christ. He was always using this phrase. "Praying always for you." Paul this has become a continuous habit to practice what he preached.

Since we heard of your faith in Christ Jesus. Because Paul heard of the faith of the Colossians Christians in Christ Jesus, he came to the conclusion that there were no secret believers among them. Paul simply refers to their faith, not as their great faith, abounding faith, or their extraordinary faith, but as the faith that was in Christ Jesus alone.

This means that they trusted in the Lord Jesus, committed themselves to Christ, and held a real vital spiritual connection with Him. Their faith was Christ-centered and was very restful in Him, and their anchor held very strong in Christ. And of the love there of; This love that he speaks of is a fruit of the spirit, as seen in: Gal. 5: 22, Rom, 5: 5. This love is the evidence or proof of faith, (St. John 13: 35, 15: 12, Gal. 5: 6, Rom. 5: 5, James 2: 14 – 20, 1John 3: 14) Love is the characteristic mark of true Christianity, it is not the superficial friendliness as some would have believed, it is to all saint.

The love that was to all saints made them not isolationists, there were no sectarian limitations. They loved everyone, of whatever disposition or position they may be in. This speaks of the depth of brotherly fellowship and the fullness of brotherly concern. They were not indifferent to the needs of others, nor disapproving of the deeds of others. In other words, they show interest in each other and they are not critical of the motives of others, no, but rather watch out for one another by giving encouragement in faith and love.

The hope states the cause or reason of their love that was laid up in heaven for them.

This means that it's stored up like a treasure, reserved, precious, and holy (2 Tim. 4:8, 1 Pet. 1:3-5). The hope that Paul speaks about is still the future and its nature is still unknown, but its possession is absolutely sure and certain. Where have they heard all things about love and hope before? Be sure that the quarters that they heard it from did not give true meaning to it. But they did hear the gospel from Epaphras before Gnosticism crept in. The word of truth which is the gospel of truth made them aware and they knew that this hope came through the word.

Truth is the very essence of the gospel. Paul tells them of the faith which is the beginning of the Christian life. Paul also speaks of the love that holds faith and hope together, Faith resting in the past, while hope looks to the future and anticipates the crowing day. (1Joh.3:1-3)

Which is come unto YOU? This is present with you always in the world. At this time the gospel was spreading all over the world Roman Empire brought forth many fruits, making converts of many. The gospel was very dynamic and this speaks of the inner energy and transforming power of its message. It is unwise to look for fruits before there is life. "By their fruits, ye shall know them," (Matt. 7: 20) Increasing, Growing, and fruit-bearing are simultaneous. There is inward growth and outward expression. The outward extension of the gospel never stops. "Since the day ye heard." This fruit-bearing and growing has now begun and is now continuing. (Knowing the grace of God in truth)The grace of God was fully apprehended and should have made them immune from Gnosticism.

"As ye also learned of Epaphras." Epaphras was their teacher, he was a native of Colossae. He also was Paul's fellow servant and faithful minister of Christ.

"Who also declared," which really means to make manifest your love. This is the supernatural of John 3:16 and produced by the Holy Spirit.

INTERCESSION: (Colossians 1: 9 -14)

"For this cause." The reason for Paul's intercession is that one should not cease to pray daily and definitely. This means constantly and every day that he prayed. Filled with the knowledge of the will of God he believed that there would be an answer so he continually prays on. The need to pray continually is made available to each and every and not just the privileged few. The thoughts, feelings, and emotions are to be saturated with this knowledge of God's will. The word of knowledge here is in contrast with the knowledge of the Gnostics. This is full knowledge, super-knowledge, thorough knowledge gained by experience, and deep and accurate comprehension.

The Will of God is not theoretical but experimental and practical. Take note that it is knowledge of His will, not of all nature. We may not be able to understand and explain the Trinity, but we are expected to understand His plans and His purpose for our lives. This is the true foundation of all Christian character and conduct. The cure for Gnosticism is more knowledge of and obedience to God's will. In all wisdom which makes practical and good sense, this is the ability to use the knowledge which we gained from Him. This is a spiritual understanding, or spiritual insight, correct apprehension, inner perception, and clear discernment.

(i) "That ye might walk worthy." To the end that ye should walk worthy. Don't allow yourself to be looked down upon as one of God's children and walk otherwise. This is the aim and the result of knowing God's will. Knowledge is not an end in itself and is not given to satisfy curiosity. Walk refers to a total conduct and course of life. Right knowledge is issued in the right conduct. Right conduct is never the product of wrong knowledge. I am sure that God wants His children to walk worthy so they can be a credit to Jesus, and to live in conformity to our union with Christ, also in conformity with His purpose for our lives. Our lives should always be Christ-centered (Gal. 2: 20).

Whatever we say and do should depict Christ. Unto all pleasing, this is not the pleasing of everybody, but pleasing God in everything, in every way and at all times. Being

Fruitful! This modifies the word walk. Continually bearing fruit is the Christian's way; Christians are to be perennial fruit-bearing in their ministry as leaders. In every good work we must grow, and demonstrate the fruit of the right relationship to Christ because this is evidence of discipleship, (John 15:8) Increasing in the knowledge of God, seeing God by faith, and searching out His will day after day will help one in knowing God. This also speaks of both the sphere where spiritual growth takes place and spiritual growth. According to (2 Peter 3:18) a fruit-bearing tree will always grow. And the tree that does not grow or ceases to bear fruit will be rendered useless and cast away.

(ii) "Strengthened with all might." Empowered with all might and power we are engaged in a spiritual conflict and warfare, (Eph. 6:10) and we need this spiritual power from God in this hostile and unspiritual world to grow and bring forth fruit. The word strengthened is in the Greek present tense, and this indicates that God keeps on continuously and progressively and constantly filling us with dynamic power, according to His glorious power and His timeless Omnipotence. This strengthening is not proportioned simply to our need, but according to His abundant supply unto all. The threefold result of such empowerment is, not working miracles, not an outburst of eloquence, but producing homely virtues. Patience, literally, "remaining under" This is the opposite of cowardice and despondence.

It is forbearance, steadfast endurance, fortitude, and the capacity to see things through. It means remaining under difficulties without succumbing to them. Long-Suffering: This is the opposite of wrath and revenge. It is self-restrain, even temperance, holding out long. Long-suffering does not retaliate in spite of injury or result (cf. James 5: 7–11), with joyfulness, not with a long face, not with a sticky smile, but with a Psalm in the night. "The joy of the Lord is your strength." (Neh. 8:10)

(iii) "Giving thanks." Not striving for, not praying for, but giving thanks for three things which are, made us meet, made us fit and adequate, not worthy; He qualified us, made us competent and sufficient. This is true of every Christian. There are no degrees of fitness for special people only. Fitness depends on privilege and position, not character or experience. The Greek aorist tense points to the instantaneous act of conversion, not a progressive process. It is a present reality to be made partakers of the inheritance, not as purchasers. We have a portion and share of the inheritance as an unearned gift, in the light that marks the inheritance as future and as heavenly. Light speaks of the realm where there is no light and no sin.

(iv) "Delivered us from the power of darkness." God rescued or liberated us all from the power, dominion, authority, and tyranny of darkness. This darkness speaks of a miserable or horrible state of being. One who is held captive by Satan? Darkness then is a symbol of ignorance, falsehood, and sin. Translated as "us", this is an accomplished fact that God transported, transplanted, and transferred us from the devil's dominion to be under Christ's control. To be in the kingdom of His dear Son. We are aware that the Son is the object of the Father's love. Paul rules out the system of acorns which the Gnostics placed above Christ. It is Christ's kingdom that is sovereign. He is ruler over His kingdom the God who removes us from the realm of darkness and He established us as colonists and as citizens in the realm of light. (Peter 2: 9)

(v) "In whom we have Redemption". This is a present possession; we have redemption because of our union with Christ. Redemption means deliverance, ransom, release, and emancipation. Redemption also speaks of our release on the payment of a ransom, (Mark 10: 45; Acts 20:28; Gal. 3:13; Titus 2:14) "Through His Blood". The best text do not contain these words; however this truth is taught elsewhere (Eph. 1:7; 1 Peter 1:18; 1 John 1:7).

This Deliverance is exhibited by the forgiveness of sins; this is the logical result of redemption which is the real consequences of salvation. Forgiveness is remission or the sending away, removal, or casting away of all sins. It is also the erasing of our sins which will not be accounted for anymore, because of the shed blood of Jesus Christ (Micah 7:18; Isa. 43: 25; 44:22).

St. Paul being an Apostle of Jesus Christ was met by Jesus Christ himself on the road to Damascus. This came to pass while he was going on a rampage to persecute the Christians. He became very powerful and useful in the hands of the Almighty. After his conversion, he preach the unadulterated gospel without fear or favor. He also did this in season and out of season and declared that the Son of God is the object of His Father's love. He set the stage with a thankful attitude for all his followers to follow.

STUDY POINTS

- Did Paul ever refer to himself as an Apostle?

- Who was Paul to Timothy?

- Did St. Paul ever go to the Colossians' Church?

- Define the foundation of all Christian character and conduct.

- According to verse (11) of the Colossians chapter (1), why should we be strengthened with all might?

CHAPTER 4

THE PERSON AND WORK OF JESUS CHRIST - CHRISTOLOGY OF COLOSSIANS 1:15-29

Perhaps no other text in the Pauline Corpus matches the literary beauty, Christological Candor, or semantic density of Colossians 1:15-20. C. D. Moule calls it "perhaps the most striking of all the Pauline expressions of conviction as to the status of Christ. C. D. Moule[4], "Every clause is pregnant of divine truth and the whole teaches with majestic emphasis the great lesson that the Person is all-important to the work, the true Christ to the true salvation." John R. W. Scott states as he describes this passage as "a sublime statement of the absolute supremacy of Jesus Christ." E. Y. Mullins calls it "the most comprehensive[5] and exhaustive statement of

---

[4] Page 591: Liberty Bible commentary N.T. C D.Moule, perhaps the most striking of all the Pauline expressions of conviction as to "the status of Christ"

[5] Pages 591 John R.W.Scott, "a sub line statement of the absolute supremacy of Jesus Christ", Mulling. The most comprehensive.

Paul's estimate of Jesus Christ to be found anywhere in his Epistles."

In one hundred and twelve Greek words, the Apostle Paul splendidly describes the four essential aspects of the person and work of Christ. He is God and Ideal-Man, and he is revealed and Lord. This text in the context of Scripture (en toto) offers a sufficient amount of evidence to demonstrate confidently that Jesus Christ is fully divine and fully human with respect to his person. The text also demonstrates that he is the perfect revealer of God and Lord of creation and re-creation concerning his work. In other words, on the strength of this one text, interpretation in light of all Scripture can be shown that Jesus Christ is God, Ideal-Man, Revealer, and Lord of all creation. Six key phrases will be examined to discover to what extent they support the above claims about the person and work of Christ.

Christ: The Visible Image of the Invisible God

15a. Who is the image of the image (eikon) of the invisible God: - (Eikon) is used twenty-three times in the New Testament and two times with (tou theo). When it occurs in the Septuagint it translates five Hebrew words, but (tselem) is the chief Hebrew word behind (eikon) (Eikon) generally means "likeness." C. Moule observes, however, that the context makes it clear that Paul has applied (eikon) here "in a unique way."

The Greeks used (eikon) to mean an "artistic representation" in the strict sense and a "mental image" in the metaphorical sense. In this sense, a "copy" (eikon) means a "living image," a "likeness," an "embodiment" and a "manifestation." Gerhard Kittel remarks, "All the emphasis is on the equality of the (eikon) with the original... The being of Jesus as the image is only another way of talking about his being as the Son.

There are two aspects of meaning representation and manifestation. H. Moule, (eikon) connotes similarity, representation, derived likeness, and manifestation. As he states in the (BLC page 591)[1], "The Lord Christ, in the mystery of his Person and Natures, is not only a Being resembling God, but God Manifest." And F. F. Bruce interprets (eikon) in the following way: To call Christ the image of God is to say that in him the being and nature of God have been perfectly manifested--that in him the invisible has become visible.

Murray J. Harris admits that the meaning of (eikon) is not fixed outside its context, but in this context, it refers to exact likeness. He suggests (eikon) could range in meaning "from a partial or superficial resemblance to a complete or essential likeness. Given 1:19; 2:9, (eijkw) signifies that Jesus is an exact, as well as a visible, representation of

God." Otto Flender defines (eikon) in a way that depicts exact likeness as well. He writes, "There is no difference here between the image and the essence of the invisible God. In Christ we see God."

Oscar Cullmann, links (eikon) with (morphe) an equivalent Pauline term that expresses the deity of Christ. He also links these Pauline terms with the (logos)" of John.19 He writes, "The designation 'image of God' (Col. 1.15) . . . implies Jesus' deity just as clearly as does the title logos" in John 1:1.

Moule Book Liberty Commentary

While several commentators define (eikon) in a way that emphasizes the deity of Christ, others see its value in asserting the humanity of Christ as well. C. Moule makes such a connection between 15a and the humanity of Christ: "If Man is 'in the image of God' . . . then so is Christ par excellence. He is the perfect likeness of God." * (Moral attributes vs. Natural attributes).

N. T. Wright also makes a clear defense for the complete humanity and deity of Christ.

He asserts that this text "refers to the exalted man, but identifies him with the pre-existent Lord." He writes, that the true humanity of Jesus is the climax of the history of creation, and at the same time the starting point of the new creation. From all eternity Jesus had, in his very nature, been the 'image of God', reflecting perfectly the character and life of the Father. It was thus appropriate for him to be the 'image of God' as man. The doctrine of incarnation which flows from this cannot, by definition, squeeze either 'divinity' or 'humanity' out of shape.

The evidence suggests that the (eikon) phrase of 15a means that Jesus Christ is the uniquely visible, humanly divine, exact representation and manifestation of God, who cannot otherwise be seen by mortal men. This being the case, Christ Himself and no other is the perfect revelation of what God and ideal man are like. For in his humanity, Jesus is exactly like pre-fallen Adam who was made in the image of God, and in His deity, Jesus is exactly like God who made Adam in His image. Since Christ is God then it follows that he is Lord-Creator over all creation, and since he is both God and the Ideal-man then it follows that he is the perfect mediator between the creator and fallen creation. He is also, therefore, Lord-Recreator of fallen creation.

Christ: The Firstborn—Prior to and Priority over all creation (who is) the firstborn over all creation: (Prototokos) is used rarely outside the Bible and does not occur at all before the Septuagint. Of about one hundred and thirty occurrences in the Septuagint, many stress the relative importance of the firstborn. It is often used in the Old Testament to reflect a special position with reference to God, or supremacy of rank. Prototokos occurs eight times in the New Testament in the singular and each time it is used exclusively with reference to Jesus Christ.

According to Wilhem Michaelis, the expression of 15b "does not simply denote the priority in time of the pre-existent Lord." Based on v.16, "Christ is the Mediator at creation to whom all creatures without exception owe their creation. . . . It cannot be said at the same time that he was created as the first creature." Karl H. Bartels asserts, "As a title of honor for Jesus, (Prototokos) expresses more clearly than almost any other the unity of God's saving will and acts. . . . Creator and Redeemer are one and the same. . . . In the man Christ Jesus, the (Prototokos), God has brought his divine power and glory to its climax (Col. 1:19f.).

Moule admits that without a context it might be natural to understand (Prototokos) with the Arians: describing Christ as the eldest among created things. But this interpretation is "inconsistent" with v.16 and the following. Moule, (Prototokos) incorporates both time and supremacy with "a little more to be said in favor" of supremacy.

Others join C. Moule and appropriate both ideas of time and rank to this (Prototokos) phrase. F. F. Bruce suggests that this use of (Prototokos) speaks of Christ's pre-existence and cosmic activity in creation. "(Prototokos) with the genitive has the same force that (protos) with the genitive has in John 1:15, 30: it denotes not only priority but primacy." Wright also interprets this phrase as an expression of the priority of time and supremacy of rank, together with H. Moule, Lightfoot, Harris, and Curtis Vaughan. H. Moule suggests that (Prototokos) denotes priority of existence, so that "the Son appears as antecedent to the created Universe" and denotes Lordship over all creation by His "right of eternal primogeniture."

Richard Melick, however, and G. B. Caird prefer to interpret this (Prototokos) phrase without reference to time. Melick writes, "Therefore the point is that Jesus is the firstborn (preeminent) with reference to the creation just as Paul argued that Jesus was preeminent "out of the dead." And Caird asserts that (Prototokos) in both occurrences denotes "status and sovereignty" with no sense of "temporal priority."

The evidence suggests that this (Prototokos) phrase as amplified by verse 16 means that Jesus Christ exclusively enjoys a special title of honour and a special relationship with God. As (Prototokos) over all creation, Christ is the uncreated creator. He is prior in time to all creation and he is the supreme Lord over all creation. Christ is prior to and exercises priority over the entire cosmos. He reigns over all creation with the highest undisputable status and sovereignty because he is its creator.

If Christ creates then Christ is God because only God creates. His work as creator is extremely strong evidence of His deity. And since creation is a visible manifestation of the creator's person and work, then Christ's work of creation is a profound demonstration that he is also the perfect revealer of what God who cannot be seen is like.

Man does not create, however. So this phrase may not be used as evidence for the humanity of Christ. The redemptive work of Christ is not yet in view (see v. 18) so this occurrence of (Prototokos) may not serve to support directly Jesus' role as Lord over the new creation.

Christ: Pior to and Priority over all things

He is before all things: (Pros) is a very common preposition that means "before," "in front of," or "at" with reference to place. It can also mean "before" with reference to time. And (pros) may mean "above" with reference to precedence, rank, or advantage. It is more commonly used with reference to place or time. According to Herbert Preisker and Siegfried Schulz this use of pros) means: Christ existed "before all things," the pre-existence of Christ here is not a speculative theology but a dynamic expression of the unrestricted world dominion of [Christ].

Some writers find only a temporal quality in this expression and others find only supremacy, while still others find elements of both. For example, Lightfoot and Hendriksen ascribe only a "temporal priority" to this phrase while Caird asserts "the absolute and universal priority [in rank] of Christ" based on the present tense verb. Caird writes, "We are not told that Christ existed before the world began, but that he is before all things." Harris, Vaughan, and Wright find both aspects of time and rank with rank as the more prominent concept.

Moule notes four possible interpretations in consideration of the possible dual meaning of the preposition and the presence of the verb (ejstin) with (pros) -- "he exists before," "he exists as supreme over," "he is before," and "he is supreme over." Moule prefers "he exists before" which would make him an advocate of (pros) interpreted with reference only to time.

Perhaps the (pros) expression is designed to complement and reinforce the context of Christ's work as Lord of creation. It emphasizes the pre-existence of Christ slightly more. While the Prototokos apparently stresses the idea of rank but includes indirectly the aspect of time, the (pros) phrase here apparently stresses the idea of priority in time but includes indirectly the aspect of rank.

The evidence suggests that the pros means that Christ existed before [in time] everything was created, therefore it follows that he ranks supremely over all he creates. Jesus Christ is the exclusive Lord of creation. Only God creates, so Christ is God. Creation manifests the Creator, so He is the Revealer of God. But this phrase remains quiet on the matter of Christ's humanity and his role in re-creation.

Christ: The Firstborn - Prior to all others in the resurrection

(who is) the firstborn from the dead: - The semantic possibilities are the same for (prototokosin)

For the same reasons offered above, but the immediate context reshapes the interpretation of this phrase. (Prototokos) may denote priority with reference to time, rank, or both. In 15b, (Prototokos) refers to "all creation," but 18c refers to "from the dead." Whereas the former occurrence had to do with Christ's Lordship over creation this occurrence has to do with His Lordship over re-creation. In other words, Christ is depicted as the One who ranks first above the entire creation because he is the Creator. But, in this phrase, Christ is depicted as the One who ranks first above the entire re-creation, or what H. Moule calls "the whole spiritual creation."

Christ: The Humanly Divine Reconciler Mediator Of All Creation:

"Through Him to reconcile all things unto Himself." The key term is (apokatalaxia) its roots are (apokatalasso) and is not found prior to the New Testament or outside Ephesians and Colossians. According to Friedrick Buchsel the meaning and use of (apokatalasso) are "basically the same as those of (katalosso") which denotes a transformation or renewal of the state between God and man and therewith of man's needy state. The usage in 20a may be taken to mean the being created in Christ, (Col. 1: 16). There we'll be found in Him as the Head, (Col. 2: 10) so that the reconciliation of all things will lead to their subjection to Christ even when they are not fully in Him.

Christ; Unique and Efficient Re–Creator:

The strongest evidence in this passage for the redeeming work of Christ as an efficient reconciler of creation or in other words efficient Lord Re–Creator is found in the (aipokatallavvxai) phrases (V20a) and the phrase (18a). Jesus Christ is the efficient peacemaking mediator between God and all fallen men, and between God and his fallen creation, because he is both God and man. He is the creator and the inhabitant of creation. Christ makes this peace with God on behalf of all creation through his substitutionary death on the cross. He makes the re-creation and reconciliation of man possible through his shed blood, his spots upon him, his stripes, and the whipping he bore. He fell while carrying the cross up to Calvary Hill for all mankind. He also models re-creation through his resurrection.

Now, who do I say that Jesus Christ the Son of Man is? I confidently declare it is true, yes certainly true; even ultimately true that Jesus Christ is the Son of the Living God! He is the express image of the invisible God, the firstborn of all creation, the firstborn from the resurrection, and the reconciliations of one of all things. He is my God my Ideal- man, my Revealer, and my Lord. May He become yours, quit soon, open your eyes, and see him clearly. Open your hearts and serve him fully.

In Philippians 2: 5 – 11 it says, "Let this mind be in you which was in Christ Jesus…. That at the name of Jesus, every knee shall bow and every tongue shall confess that Jesus Christ is Lord. Everyone must recognize Jesus Christ as Lord and bow to Him. Some may do this voluntarily, while others may not, but he is Lord anyway and must be treated as such. There is only one God and one mediator between God and man, the man Christ Jesus. He is the Godhead (Trinity) in the flesh. He was in the creation, for by Him were all things created, that are in the heavens and that are under the earth, visible and invisible. Things we can see and that which we cannot see. Therefore He's Lord over all domain because he owns everything.

STUDY POINTS

- Give proof that Jesus is Lord of Creation.

- How do you know that Jesus was born of the Godhead?

- Give three other names that Jesus was classified as.

- How did Jesus Christ abolish the Law?

- Give evidence that Jesus was not just the Son of God.

CHAPTER 5

THE POSITION OF THE CHURCH IN JESUS CHRIST (COL. 2: 1 – 15)

St. Paul had to focus his mind straight before him in order to reach the goal. He also was assisted greatly by divine energy and power from God to help him. He suffered intense struggles, (like an athlete in the race) agonizing in strength. But in spite of it all he had to keep strong for the church. Paul was God's instrument in his work, through his power and for his glory.

Paul's Loving Care (Col. 1: 28, ch. 2 : 3) Knew Loving Care:

Paul's desire for the church at Colossae was for the church to know the seriousness of the situation and the perils that Paul had to stand up to for their sake. He wanted them to also know that they could appreciate him, pray for him, and share with him in this great conflict. The strain of Paul's soul could be seen had he carried out his pastoral concern (II Cor. 11: 28; I Thes.2:2). For you, the Colossians, Laodiceans, and for the other churches, Paul very earnestly prayed for the converts and for the churches.

In Colossians 1 vs.2: Hearts...... comforted confirmed, strengthened, encouraged, not consoled but strengthened not relief, but reinforcement. They were in danger of being shaken, being knitted together in love. A closer unity, a vital helpful relationship, being welded together, united. This will help us to be safely guarded against the corruption and the disruption of false teachings. All riches complete abundance of inward wealth: Full assurance, confidence, deep conviction, and full knowledge of Christ, (1 Cor. 2: 12; Eph. 3:17 – 20), to the acknowledgment and personal knowledge of the secret.

In Colossians 1 vs.3: In who are hidden, Paul told them not to look anywhere else, but in Christ, because our thesaurus or storehouse of treasures is in Christ Jesus. The treasures are available and accessible to every believer. Paul comforts the Gnostics with the fact that Christ sums up all wisdom and knowledge.

The Threatening Danger: False Philosophy Col. 2: 4 -7:

"Beguile", Literally, "Reason and alongside." This means to elude, deceive by false reasoning and lead astray, (Matt. 24:4; Acts 20:30; 1 Cor. 11:13; Eph. 4:14, 1 Joh.4:1)

These are enticing words, attractive arguments, persuading rhetoric, plausible speech, fast talk, and a smooth line.

In Colossians 2 vs.5 "Your order", is a military term, (Gr. taxis) indicating an orderly array of disciplined soldiers. The Colossian's ranks had not been broken yet, but the Gnostics were attacking and Paul was concerned about them. The steadfastness of your faith in Christ. Another military word (Gr. Sterioma) signifies solitude with unbroken ranks, every man was in his right place, as they presented a solid front. This however speaks of the unyielding nature of their faith which was firm and true to Christ.

In Colossians 2 vs.6 "As…..received Christ Jesus the Lord." This refers to a personal appropriation of Christ. We are not just believing a truth about Him as Paul described, but using the unique phrase, Paul discharges both barrels at the same time to correct the two forms of Gnostic heresy about the person of Christ (1) The recognition of the historical Jesus in his actual humanity, (Docetic Gnostics) and (2) The identity of Christ with historical Jesus, (Cerinthian Gnostics). So walk, live accordingly, and keep on walking. Our walk must match our talk, In other words, walk the walk, and talk the talk, and please the Lord Jesus Christ.

In Colossians 2 vs.7 "Rooted"; is permanently rooted in Christ and firmly anchored in Him. We should stay put and not be easily shaken. This is what God has done, "built up" This is a continual process, being built up constantly is like an ever-expanding building that is built up block by block until one meets their goal. We go from one level to another in Him. "Established in the Faith", means to make firm or stable. "Abounding" is the natural consequence.

The Saving Doctrine Of Jesus Christ Col. 2:8–15.

In Colossians 2 vs.8 "Beware" Take heed, be on your guard, keep a watchful eye, always be open, and be alert to the imminent danger because the enemy is lurking in the darkness. His aim is to spoil you, carry you away into captivity, or carry you off as booty. This picture that is given is like kidnapping you for the purpose of seducing you against having faith in Christ. It is not just robbing you of some blessing, but taking you as a captive, which gives a picture of being a long-time prisoner of war, as you are being led away into slavery. The false teachers were men-stealers entrapping and dragging men into spiritual slavery.

"Through philosophy," Love of wisdom, Paul does not condemn knowledge and wisdom, but only this false philosophy, knowledge falsely named (1 Tim.6:2) and vain deceit. An explanation of this philosophy is empty delusions, vain speculations hollow sham, devoid of truth, high-sounding nonsense. This all amounts to nothing, and cannot meet the needs of the soul, or answer the questions that are in one's mind. "After the tradition of men". This means that which is handed down. Here it refers to the foolish theories of the Gnostics. We see here a contrast between human reason and divine revelation, (Mark 7: 6 – 9); man's theories versus God's truth, or fables versus facts. "After the rudiments of the world," This means, anything in a row or series, (Gr. Stoicheion) like a letter of the alphabet, elementary, preparatory, and immature. Paul is speaking of the ritualistic and materialistic, which are elements of Gnosticism.

This really is a contrast between the outward and the material as opposed to the inward and the spiritual. "And not after Christ", In contradiction to Christ and to God's word Gnosticism stood in the way of Christ, it really weakened faith in Christ, took away the eyesight from looking to and at Christ, and also took men away from the Christ of Calvary. Such heresy is best met, not by detailed discussion, not by little denunciation but by the declaration of truth.

In Colossians 2 vs.9 "For in Him" This is emphatic, and means nowhere else, "Dwelled". Permanent residence. All attributes and the essence of deity are in Christ, not just divinity or in other words, divine, but deity, not just Godlike but God, God in reality and not a nature like Gods, but a nature the same as Gods. "Bodily". The incarnation was real. it was not a story to tell or a fairy tale. It really happened through the instrumentality of the Blessed Holy

Ghost. Here our Lord Jesus Christ was one person with two natures; God and man. Paul disposes of the Docetic theory, "that Jesus has no human body, as well as the Corinthians theory separation between the man Jesus and acorn Christ means the long period between Jesus the man Jesus the Christ. Paul declares the deity and the humanity of Jesus Christ in corporeal form.

In Colossians 2 vs.10 "And ye are complete in Him". God did this in connection with Christ. This is both complete and permanent. Having been completely filled in the past we are in a state of fullness now, and all we need is in Christ. We will seek no other source of grace and truth; we show no allegiance to anyone else, and will submit to no other authority; Jesus is the head; He is the source of all life, and is sovereign over all life

In Colossians 2 vs.11 "Circumcised" This aspect truly points to conversion. (Rom. 4:1; ch. 2: 28–30, Phil.3:3). The character of this circumcision is spiritual and physical. It is without hands inward and not outward, the extent of this circumcision is the body and not just one organ. The author of this circumcision is Christ, not Moses. This circumcision that Paul speaks of is not a rite or a ceremonial act, but in reality, "Putting off of the body which is the flesh. Stripping off or casting aside as a filthy piece of clothing or garment". The flesh should be removed from the throne of one's life and the Christian then will be free from his sinful nature. The evil nature will not be eradicated according to (1 John 1:8) but its power is broken. Christ is now on the throne and our physical members are to be instruments not of unrighteousness onto sin, but righteousness unto God. (Rom. 6:11-14).

In Colossians 2 verse 12 "Buried with Him in Baptism" "Buried with him in baptism", jointly entombed with Christ, sharing in his experience. We then apply baptism outward as a sign. God provides the reality of inward union with Christ. In this, we say that circumcision without hands (God's work) is the same as God's baptism union with Christ.

In Colossians 2 vs.13 "And you, being dead". This means that one is devoid of the life of Christ or life in God, and one is left with a totally depraved nature, (Eph. 2: 1, ch. 5:6 & 11). Has he been quickened, made alive in union with Christ? You became able to be free with strength from God, having forgiven you all your trespasses. Yes, graciously pardoning, canceling, and erasing the debt, (cf. Luke 7:42)

In Colossians 2 vs.14 Blotting out, erasing, wiped out, obliterated, and cancelled the note. This explains the forgiveness; the handwriting of ordinances; and the handwritten document consisting of ordinances. The bond here is the certification of debt, the instrument of condemnation, the indictment drawn up against the prisoner, and a signed confession of indebtedness.

Three expressions describe the law. (1) It is written in ordinance, expressed in decree and commandments; (2) It was against us, and had a valid claim on us; (3) It was contrary to us because we could not meet the claim. Paul states that bond was: (1) blotted out; (2) taken out of the way; (3) nailed to His cross. This was a once for all removal (1 Cor. 5:21; Eph. 2:15-16; Gal. 3:13). In the East, a bond is canceled by nailing it to the post. Our bond of guilt was nailed to his cross.

"In Colossians 2 vs. 15 "Having spoiled principalities and powers" Stripped off and away from, the principalities and powers are conquered antagonists stripped of their weapons and disarmed. (Matt. 12:29; Luke 11:21–22; John 16:11; Rom. 8:37–39; 1 Cor.15:55–57; Heb. 2:4) By His death Christ has conquered all His enemies, stripped them of their powers, exposed them to public disgrace, held them up in contempt and led them captives in His triumph and victory over them.

St. Paul loved the church very much and so he suffered a lot for it. His wish was for them to know the depth of his suffering so that they would appreciate the sacrifices he was making and the enduring sacrifice for the struggles he was under. All these were because of the love and devotion he had for the church at Colossae. Paul wanted the church to be rooted and grounded in truth and in Christ so that nothing would be able to shake and move them where the love of God is concerned. He also wanted them to be closely knitted together as saints in Christ, and that there would be no loophole for the enemy to creep in, and create havoc among them.

Paul's loving care for the Colossian Church made him stand up for the faith and convictions that they were living for. He would pray earnestly and continuously for them that they would walk the walk, and talk the talk, where their devotion to Christ Jesus is concerned. He also comforted and strengthened them in their journey as Christians. He encouraged them to be permanently rooted in Christ and to be stabilized in the faith. He shows them how they can be firmly built up in their faith in the Lord Jesus Christ. Paul told them that where circumcision is concerned, it is spiritual and not physical. It is without hands, it is inward and outward. Therefore the flesh is removed from the throne of the heart and by this, the Christian is made free from the sinful nature.

Study Points

- In all of Paul's suffering what was his main reason for his endurance?

- Describe the Christian walk as Paul would have the Colossians do.

- What was Paul's warning to the Colossians that they should beware of?

- What is the circumcision that Paul speaks of so glowingly?

- What our physical members are to be as Paul says?

CHAPTER 6

THE RESPONSIBILITY OF THE CHURCH TO BELIEVERS: (COLOSSIANS 2: 16 - 23)

At this stage, the Church has the charge to every believer to see to it that each one does walk in the way of truth. In other words, the Church should see to it that each one is his brother's keeper in the faith, helping each person to walk well. The Church should be in a position to see the dangers of beguiling members who are weaker in the faith and are easily carried away, to the worshiping of angels and any other thing that will be displeasing to our God. The Church should also be looking out for those persons who are not or non-members of the body who have made decisions to see that they don't turn back to the things that they have left off to follow Christ, who is the head of the body and the head of the Church.

There Must Be No Submission To The Former Legalism, (Col. 2: 16 -17)

In Colossians 2 vs. 16 "Let no man therefore judge you," Sit in judgment. This means to take you to task, deciding for you, criticizing and condemning you. As we see, Paul here is encouraging the Colossian Christians not to allow themselves to be enslaved by legalism, ritualism, rites, and ceremonies. With regards to legalism which is the law, one should not allow himself to be enslaved by it so that he cannot serve God the way they should. As with ritualism, the Colossian Christians should not be tied to or chained, so that they can't obey the commands of Christ. The ceremonies and the rituals that are not necessary to salvation don't allow you to be tied to them so that they cannot see the danger or leanness in them, and that will keep them from doing the things of God, without being afraid.

In Colossians 2 vs. 17 "Which is a shadow", A shadow is not the real thing. It's an imitation of the real thing. There is a difference between the shadow and the substance. Symbols and types may stimulate thought, these may awaken emotions convey divine truth, and even strengthen faith, but beyond this, they are meaningless and dangerous and may replace the Living Christ. Mosaic institutions are of value, setting forth man's need for pardon, purity, and holiness.

The Mosaic systems also set forth God's provision of a great high priest, an atonement, and fellowship with God. Why should we look at shadow when we can look at the Christ? He is the author and the finisher of our faith. God is our maker and He knows each and everything about every one of us. He knows exactly all the things that we are in need of, when we need them, and how we need them. So it should be in our hearts to look to Him. These ceremonies are shadows, superseded, and shall be abandoned. Since Christ has come as the perfect light we no longer need symbols and types. (Heb.8: 13, ch. 10: 1). Christ now has become the real object, not an imitation; So we don't need any substitute to follow or to lead us.

There Must Be No Subservience To False Philosophy, (Col. 2: 18 – 19)

In Colossians 2 vs. 18 "Let no man beguile you of your reward," this means to rob you of your prize, rob your present, and of your possession. The word really means to act as an umpire, denying your claim of what is rightly yours, defrauding you, and declaring you as unworthy. This means that you don't deserve it.

"Voluntary humility". This means self–imposed, mock – humility which is expressed in worshiping of angels. Intruding …not seen, this refers to alleged visions imagined and invented revelations, and the living in a world of hallucination.

"Vainly puffed up". This means to be inflated with conceit, senseless pride like a big puff of wind. Fleshly minded, literally means the mind of the flesh. Such a person is dominated by his "unregenerate" nature and devoid of spiritual enlightenment. It is very difficult for such persons to give a clear interpretation of the scriptures or the word of truth because they will always interpret things to suit the flesh.

In Colossians 2 vs.19 "And not holding the Head". This is a person who lacks a vital connection with Christ and has never been a part of the body. The figure of the body emphasizes both its unity and its diversity. Christ supplies (1) nourishment, that is life and energy, (2) i.e., knitted together, and (3) growth, that is the increase of God.

Dead With Christ, We Are Free From Earthly Ordinances: (Col. 2:20–23)

In Colossians 2 vs. 20 "Wherefore if ye be dead with Christ". Now one dies at the time of their conversion, according to (Romans 6:2–4; Ch. 6: 11; Ch. 7:4; 2 Cor. 5:15; Gal. 6:14). Death means separation, and for the Colossian they were separated from the rudiments of this world. This refers to the first principle, the childish lesson, and the A.B.C's of elementary spiritual instruction. The subject of ordinances, pestered by the rules and regulations. These are outward forms; outworn, annulled, and superseded. But accepting Christ you are dead with him in his death and resurrection.

In Colossians 2 vs. 21 "Touch not, taste not, handle not." Specimens of Gnostic rules, of which the Christian stand liberated from. It refers to the discipline that the believer has to possess in his Christian character and conduct. These are still the tests of our Holiness in certain religious groups.

In Colossians 2 vs. 22 "Perish with the using," Destined by corruption in their consumption. After the weakness of man. Human origin is not based on the will and the word of man. (Matt. 15:8–9)

In Colossians 2 vs. 23 "A show of wisdom in will and worship," An appearance, a masquerading; Will worship is self-imposed worship, prescribed for one's self. Humanity, spurious, hypocritical, mock humanity.

In Colossians 2 vs. 24 "Neglecting of the body," This means, Ascetic discipline, serve, harsh, torturing, not in any honor, not of any value, impotent, not a remedy, it can't deliver. This means that it is not for any real enjoyment for anyone. The satisfying and indulgence of the flesh.

The Church must always be on the lookout for any and every opening for sin in the believer's life, also for the ways that the enemy could enter and destroy the believer or separate him from becoming what He wills him to become in Christ. Therefore the Church is there to help each one to stand firmly in Christ.

In the church, there must be no submission to form legalism in that will because they take you to judgment in deciding for you. Paul here was encouraging the Colossians not to be so caught up and be enslaved in legalism. Also, they should not be chained that they could not obey the commands of Christ, who is their Master. Then as a Church, each one should keep a watch over each other, helping to keep them from the danger of all these things. In other words, help them to keep their eyes spiritually open speaking to them regularly so that none of them fall into those things as prey to them.

STUDY POINTS

- Let no man beguile you of your rewards; Explain.

- What does death really mean in Colossians?

- When do we die with Christ?

- Why should we use symbols since Christ has come?

- Give an example of one of the false philosophies that the Colossians were warned against.

CHAPTER 7

THE RESPONSIBILITY OF THE CHURCH TO THE WORLD (COLOSSIANS 3 & 4)

Paul was encouraging the Colossians Christians to live as how Jesus Christ expected them to live, now that they were called out from the world to be children of the Most High God. They should act in all their ways depicting Christ so that as the world looks on they will see Christ who is the Head of the Church, and emulate their ways of living by His standard. Then in doing this, they would bring glory to the name of Christ. This will surely help in encouraging the people around who are not saved, to accept Christ as their risen Savior and Lord.

Risen With Christ, We Are Bound To Heavenly Principles, (Col. 3: 1 – 4)

In Colossians 3 vs.1 "If ye then be risen with Christ". Since you are now jointly raised up a new life has begun. Seek, and keep on seeking, outward active things, "Real heavenly" spiritual things (2Cor. 4: 18) "Above," The upward things, (Phil. 3: 14) "Treasures of heaven" (Matt. 6: 20) Our head is there, our home is there. Where Christ sits, the place, the place is exaltation, power, and authority, Paul gives heavenly motives for earthly duties.

In other words, Paul here is telling the Colossians, "Since you are risen up with the Colossians to think of themselves in Christ a new way, with a new status because you all were dead in trespasses and sin, look for the things that the newness of life requires, and that is found in Christ Jesus. Look for them diligently and practice them always as followers of Christ or His dear children heading for our heavenly home with him. Because the world around needs to see proof of what you believe in, what changes the new life in Christ really made in you, that causes you to possess what you are now professing. The world or the universe needs to see the changes, principles to heavenly principles their manner of living, why? because the things of heaven are real treasures and spiritual. Jesus is our head and he's always there even in hard times.

Colossians 3 vs.2 "Set your affection" This is inward and active, something to keep on thinking about and directing your mind towards heavenly things. One should have his mind set on heavenly things, the treasures of heaven. We as God's children should live and do everything in the light of eternity. The Christian must be heavenly-minded, not worrying about earthly things, yet they are still living here on earth until the time of our transferring comes to go to our new home.

Colossians 3 vs. 3 "For ye are dead" This means that you are not literally dead physically, but that you have departed from the worldly life. "Your life is hidden," This is permanently hidden, we are now locked together with Christ in security, under the protection and guidance of our Head who is Christ, and Satan cannot break the lock, because we are sealed with the blood of Jesus Christ. There is therefore no way that Satan can pass over the shed blood of Jesus Christ. He's definitely afraid of the blood of Jesus.

Colossians 3 vs. 4 "Christ our life shall appear," (John. 14: 6, Phil. 1: 24, 1 John 5:11–12) this means that "We shall also appear," or be made manifest. (1 John 5: 11 – 12)

The Practical Principles Of The Inner Life (Col. 3: 5 – 17)

In his return, we are in him now, but our union is hidden in God. Colossians 3 vs. 5 "Mortify," This term means, "To put to death quickly or crucify," The flesh must be kept in place; it must die its natural death. It must be nailed to the cross.

Fornication:

This is a perilous, prevalent, perverse sin. This is a sin that is lightly regarded by many and committed without scruples and shame. It is illicit sexual intercourse between unmarried partners; similar to but not identical to adultery, (Matt. 5:32; ch. 15:19; Mark 7:21) "Uncleanness," Impurity in thought and speech, dirty-mindedness, indecency. "Inordinate affections," This is depraved passion, or uncontrolled lust an evil desire. "Evil concupiscence," is wicked craving or sensualness beyond natural expression.

Covetousness:

This is a greedy desire to have more; an entire disregard for the rights of others. "Which is idolatry?" This is the worship of false gods, putting this in place of the true and living God.

Colossians 3 vs. 6 "For which things sake," God does not regard sin with indifference, "The wrath of God," God's vengeance and dreadful judgments that will come. "Cometh," denotes certainly and immense (John 3:18–36)

Children of Disobedience:

These are called "unbelievers". "In which ye also walked" These verses characterized their past, pagan, pre-Christian experience. They were addicted to and practiced these vices, (Eph. 2: 2, 1 Peter 4:3) "Live in them" The Greek imperfect tense implies constant conduct, the habit of existence. "But now ye have put off all these" This is to put aside and rid yourself of all these completely.

Anger:

This is an uncontrolled temper, a deep-seated emotion of ill will, or a settled feeling of habitual hate, or revengeful, resentment.

Wrath:

This is a boiling agitation fiery outburst of temper, violent fit of rage, a passionate outbreak of exasperation.

Malice:

This is a vicious disposition, depraved spite, and a willful desire to injure, cruel malignity which rejoices in the evil done to others.

Blasphemy:

This is slanderous talk, reviling, evil speaking, railing insult, reckless and bitter abuse. "Filthy communications out of your mouth," which is obscene speech, shameful speaking, foul–mouthed abuse. Dirty epithets, unclean stories, (Eph. 4:29; ch.5:4)

Lie Not One to Another:

This is in the Greek present imperative tense. Forbids a continuation of action that is going on, "Stop lying" (Eph. 4: 25) There is no such thing as a little white lie; all lies are big and black. Speak the truth at all times the whole truth and not half is required but all of it. If half of the truth is spoken that's not the whole truth. Then the old man will use the other half to fight against us and seek to re-capture us again. Seeing that you have put off the old man. The old man is the old un-regenerated nature derived from Adam and Eve and received by the firstborn. The old man has not yet been converted, has not been renewed, and has not been improved.

The old man is corrupt, useless, and must be put off. The word "put off" means to strip off and discord like a filthy, worn-out garment or a piece of clothing, tossed on the rubbish heap, or to be emptied at the dumps.

"And have put on the new man," You have clothed yourself with the new man, which is Christ in you. The new man is the person you are after having been saved. The new man is the man who received Christ at the time of the second birth. At the time of the second birth that's when the regenerated man appeared with a new nature.

Renewed:

This is in the present passive participle tense in the Greek its (anakaines) which indicates constantly being renewed. This is a continuous process; the new man has not yet matured and is still in a state of development.

"Where there is neither Greek nor Jews." In the man, there is an obliteration of distinction. National privilege has been obliterated; ceremonial standings have been obliterated, cultural standing has been obliterated, and social castes have been obliterated. Christ is all and in all. Yes, Christ is absolutely everything.

Virtues to put on (Colossians 3: 12 – 17)

Colossians 3 vs.12 "Put on therefore or clothe yourself with," This is in the Greek aorist tense, imperative implies a sense of urgency. This command is to be obeyed at once. This command calls for immediate action, without delay;

we now have a characterization of believers; (1) "elect of God" which means chosen of God, (2) "Holy" which means, set apart by God and for God. (3) "Beloved" This is loved by God. These are the attire of the new man, his spiritual wardrobe of practical righteousness. "Bowels of mercies," This is one with a heart of compassion, or mercy in action, and heartfelt sympathy for the less fortunate. "Kindness" This is the thoughtfulness of others, unselfishness, a sweetness of disposition, gentleness, and graciousness. These are the fruits of the Holy Spirit and refer to the inner attitude.

"Humbleness of mind" This refers to the outward expression of that inner attitude. Humbleness is modesty it places self last and regards self as least (Eph.3: 8). "Meekness." Not weakness, but lowliness delicate consideration for others. It is the opposite of arrogance and self–assertion. Pride has no place in the Christian life. "Long-suffering" This is patient under provocation; this denotes restraint which enables one to bear injury and insult without resorting to retaliation. It accepts the wrong without complaining. Long–suffering is an attribute of God (Romans 2: 4) and a fruit of the Holy Spirit, (Gal. 5; 22) These can only be possessed by Christians who are directly sold out to Christ Jesus, those who are being led and directed by Him.

"Forbearing one another," Refers to putting up with things we dislike and getting along with those with whom we disagree. Christians can disagree without being disagreeable. This is really not an easy test, to put up with things we don't want to or things we don't like, and also to get along with those who disagree with us. However with God in your heart and mind, you are well able to do it with gracefulness. "Forgiven one another", The word forgiving in Greek is (charizomai) and is built on the same root as the word grace and means to bestow favor unconditionally. In other words, do it without any strings attached or without looking for any benefit for yourself personally. This means that Christians will always treat the offending party graciously. The Christian not only forgives but forgets. "Quarrel" Refers to a cause of blame, a ground for complaint, he thinks of himself as aggrieved.

"And above all these things," or on top of all these things, like an outer garment. "Put on Charity or Love," Love is the basis and cloak of all the graces, (1 Cor. 13: 13) "Bond" The bond that binds the other together. "Perfectness," means completeness, full grown, or mature. This also means the finished product, is a job well done.

"Let the peace of God" Better yet, the peace of Christ, this is that heart – peace which Christ demonstrated. It is a tranquility of the soul which is not ruffled up by adversity nor disturbed by fear. This peace passeth all understanding (Phil. 4: 7) and is given by Christ. (John 14:27) "Rule" refers to one who sits as umpire, arbitrates, decides all doubts settles all questions, and makes the final decision, in hearts, thoughts, feelings, and desires. "Thankful," Grateful, Appreciative.

"Let the word of Christ dwell in you richly in all wisdom," which is to be at home and dwell permanently. "With all its fullness all the time," (Josh. 1:8; John 15:7) let the word of Christ saturate you and remain in you as a rich treasure. To be added let Christ himself dwell in you with all his fullness, power, and sweetness, so that others will see the great values of the heavenly treasures in you.

"Do all in the name of the Lord Jesus," In all the relations of our lives, act as his representative, act as his ambassador, obey his word, trust in his power rely on him, and develop in his service. We all should live a Christ-centered life; all of our lives must be as Christians. Belief relates to behavior, creed, and issue in conduct, and doctrine relates to duty. Therefore, whatever your belief in Christ, let it be the duty you perform to his glory and honor.

Precepts For The Outer Life Help meets And Husbands (Colossian 3; 18 – 19)

Colossians 3 vs.18 "Wives, submit" This is an old military figure of speech, in Greek, the word is (Gr. Hypotasso) meaning to line up under (Eph. 5:22) or to subject yourself to a specialized way. There is no hint of inferiority, but a matter of authority and responsibility in the home. Wives are to be in habitual subjection with implicit trust. This is voluntary, and not to be forced on her by a demanding despot. The wives are to be helped meet, (a help that is suitable to her husband) not slaves. The family is held together by authority and obedience, and the wife's submission is prompted by the husband's love. And this fit in with our Lord's command, and should be becoming proper. In other words, this is expected of all and is to be lived in fellowship with Christ. God is really emphasizing responsibility, not rights. (Eph. 5:22-24)

Colossians 3 vs. 19 "Husbands, love your wives," or keep on loving your wives. Be consistent in your love for your wife. This is more than human affection; this love is produced by the Holy Ghost. The dominant trait of the Christian husband is self-devotion, not self-satisfaction, (Eph. 5:25–28) "Be not bitter against them," Stop being nagging and ungrateful against them. Stop being bitter and do not have the habit of being bitter against them. This sin has wrecked many marriages.

Families And Fathers (Colossian 3; 20 – 21)

Colossians 3 vs. 20 "Children, obey your parents in all things," This is an old verb, and means to listen under, harkens, to hear and to heed, to obey. Children are to have the habit of hearing and heeding instruction, (Eph.6: 1–3) in all things that pertained to Christ, this to be continual, not just occasional obedience, but all the time. This is well-pleasing for this is your commendable duty as children. This is satisfying and well done unto the Lord. In doing so there will be peace and restfulness between the children and their God, knowing that they are being obedient to the Lord's command.

Colossians 3 vs. 21 "And ye Fathers provoke not your children to wrath," this refers to the example of not producing the habit of exasperating your children. This is an old word, in Greek it's word,(Gr. Erethizo) and means to excite, not to nag, not to vex, not to rouse to resentment, (Eph. 6: 4) Fathers exasperate their children by; being inconsiderate, being too demanding and being over-corrective and being unjust and severe. Parents provoke their children by continual fault-finding, always frowning at them, never smiling, and holding up other children as examples. This action will cause their children to think of themselves as no good and that they will never amount to anything or anyone important. The twig or child is to be bent with caution, not broken lest they become discouraged. The negative purpose with the Greek present subjunctive, (Gr. Antymeo) implies the forbidding of beginning an act. Discourage means disheartened, depressed, and frustrated. Children like these are broken in spirit very easily. When broken they are quick to give up, feeling that it is impossible to please anyone.

This could well be the reason or source of the sorrow of so many and one reason why we have so many runaway children.

Servants And The Served (Colossian 3:22; ch. 4:1)

"Servants, obey in all things your masters" Paul does not denounce slavery nor demand its violent overthrow. The slaves are a part of the household, and so they become a part of the family as far as numbering is concerned. They are without rights.

They are to constantly obey their masters and give service, not demanding their freedom, service not with eye service as men-pleasers. They are to obey their masters all the time and serve them well. Not only when their masters are in their presence, but when their backs are turned also. Do your best at all times as servants to your masters.

Also, don't do service for your masters to praise you always, they should be pleased with your service, you should remember that there is a greater master than your human master so you must give an account for the service which you have done. So do your service with singleness of heart, this is to be done literally without a fold in the heart, under which one can hide false motives. Christians are to have a genuine readiness of heart or promptness of heart and an undivided purpose, not with pretense or ulterior motive, not with half-heartedness, but being sincere, fearing God, rather, or instead of the human masters according to the flesh. The real motive of service is dreading God's displeasure.

"Heartily" This literally means, (out of the soul). Christians are to draw their souls into their work and labor cheerfully and diligently, work without grumbling as to the Lord. This is the real test of Christian service, this is to prove the Christian's type of service that he or she will offer, and how deep his convictions, and devotion to God is his Master really is.

"Knowing that…of the Lord….received the reward … inheritance". The heavenly inheritance is full recompense in return for the faithful service. For ye serve the Lord Christ, and so Christians are actually employed by Christ. This is a verb and can either be indicative or an imperative intense, in which case it would mean, "keep on slaving for the Lord," It is better to be worn-out for God than to be rusted out doing nothing.

"But he that doeth wrong," Slaves or Masters, God will pay either one; there is no respect for persons. Literally, we should not be receiving people by face, or judging on the basis of out-wards appearances. There is respect for persons with man, but not with God, God does not have a double standard, He weighs the unfaithfulness in servants as well as the unkindness in masters on the same scale of divine equity and justice. God is a God of justice and there is no favoritism with Him, also there are no partialities or exceptions with Him. (1 Peter 1:17)

Colossians 4 vs.1 "Masters! Give your servant that which is just equal," This is to render on your part that which is right and fair; or to deal equitably. This would solve a lot of problems between management and labor. If we would deal justly with each other there would be no need for any quarrel between us as human beings. Knowing that we have a Master in heaven and a reminder that God keeps His eyes on the character and the conduct of all men and that every one of us shall give an account for himself to his God. (Romans 14:12)

Relation To The World (Colossians 4:2 – 6, (a) Duty of Prayer Col. 2:2–4)

"Continue in prayer," This is an appeal to give constant attention to prayer. Don't stop, do not cool off, just go on. The Christian should persevere steadfastly in intercession. (Eph. 6:18, Phil. 4:6) "Watch in the same."

This literally means to keep awake or to give strict attention to and be spiritually alert, give serious concern, and be more alert and tactful about spiritual things. Also, guard against wandering thoughts, and keep your mind steady. Don't allow your thoughts to run away with you everywhere because of indifferences. (Matt. 26:41). "With Thanksgiving," the heart should be thankful, always giving thanks to God.

"Withal praying for us," At the same time. (Eph. 6:18–19) That God would open, only God can open, (1 Cor. 6:7–9; Rom. 3:7) "A door," a door for the word, not the door of the prison. Paul is asking them to pray that he will have the opportunity to proclaim the word of God. (1 Cor. 6:16; 2 Cor. 2:12) The mystery of Christ, as opposed to the senseless mysteries of the Gnostics for which I am also in bond. Paul is conscious that his chains are the result of preaching Christ. Paul is kept in prison but he has opportunities to witness. (Phil. 1:12).

"That I may make a manifest," Paul's chief concern is to make the message clear and plain. That is, to allow all to be able to see and hear that they will be straying from the truth. As I ought to speak, as it is my duty, as it is necessary for me to speak. (1 Cor. 2:4; 2 Cor. 2:14–17).

Duty Of Propriety (Colossian 4:5–6)

"Walk in Wisdom towards them that are without". It takes wise walking as well as wise talking to win the loss to Christ. The walk refers to one's behavior. Christians are to conduct themselves wisely, not fools who do not know what he or she is doing or where he or she is going. He must speak words of wisdom, not idly throwing words around without considering their implications or the consequences of them all. The Christians must conduct themselves in ways that will leave no question marks on their lives pertaining to their Christianity. Also as they look at the times in which we are living, they should see to it that they live just like Christ.

Therefore in order to carry out the cause of Christ, we must work consistently and avoid anything that would eventually turn the unsaved off, and do everything that would turn the unsaved on and give them hope. In other words, we who are named the name of Christ and are singled out as his must walk in Christ in closeness and not mix our salvation with the things of the world in order not to be spotted with those things that are of the flesh. In doing this, we will be able to influence the unsaved to look at us and admire our lives. Then they will also be able to evaluate the validity of our walk with Christ, and come and walk with Christ too.

"Again, as pertaining to redeeming of the time," we should buy up the time, in Greek the word is (Gr. Exagorazomai) or the opportunity for one's self. We should make wise and sacred use of every opportunity we get, to the best possible advantage. We should remember that the price of self-denial and strenuous work is to be paid for or we will forego the bargain.

"Let your speech be always with grace." Christ was full of grace and truth, (John 1:14) which means that Christians are to be gracious, pleasant, attractive, winsome, and courteous. Seasoned with salt, not insipid or taste bad that will cause someone to want to vomit or spit. Not flat or dull, just tastes nice. Christians are to have an edge of liveliness and to be marked by purity or cleanness, wholesomeness, and hollowed pungency. In other words that's the Holiness of Christ and it will produce fresh taste of his glory on, in, and through us always as Christians to the unsaved. "That ye may know Him, answer every man", in order that we can adapt the message to the situation and speak appropriately to every man. This is done so that we who are saved can get used to the message of the cause and speak freely and properly or suitably to every person who questions us about our faith in Christ Jesus.

St. Paul was counseling the Colossians or the Christians in Colossae that now that they were risen with Christ, walking with Him, and in constant contact with Him, they must seek after more heavenly things because heavenly things are real and spiritual. They should also set their minds on the things pertaining to heaven. In other words, diligently search for the treasure of heaven which is so real. In doing so, they should behave themselves wisely as Christians and followers of Christ. In so doing those who are not Christians will be able to emulate them and seek to know Christ also as their Lord and Master.

COLOSSIANS

St. Paul exhorted the Colossians Christians to set their hearts and minds in heaven because they were dead to the world. In other words, they had given their whole selves to Christ and became new creatures in Christ Jesus. They were no more attached to the worldly things with their decaying attitude. They were now alive in Christ; they should now put under subjection all their members of their body and put off all the things of the world. For example; malice and wrath, which means, "a boiling agitation or fiery, out-burst of temper. This also tells of lying, they should speak the truth to one another seeing they had put off the old man which is the old unregenerate nature derived from Adam and received through the first birth

Now you have a new man which is Christ. Also, those who had masters over them, should be obedient and serve them with sincerity and respect. Children also should be obedient to their parents in all things and the blessings of the Lord will follow them. Fathers should not provoke their children to wrath, because this will get them discouraged to give up on themselves, and they will turn to other things and people who will interest them, and they will surely be led astray.

Study Points

- Since the Colossians were New Born Christians, what should they now seek after?

- 2. Now that they are dead, where are their lives?

- 3. Give three examples of the deeds that they had put away in the flesh.

- 4. Name three of the things that they should put on as dearly beloved.

- 5. Then above all things, the most important of all things that they should put on is?

CHAPTER 8

CONCLUSION (COLOSSIANS 4:7–18)

This would seem as though, Paul was doing his last round as we find him doing in this Roman imprisonment, surrounded by many of his oldest and most valued attendants. For example, we have Luke, his fellow traveler, who remained with him during his bondage. Timothy, his beloved son in the faith ministered to him at Rome as he did in Asia, in Macedonia, and Achaia. Tychicus who had formerly borne him company from Corinth to Ephesus is now at hand to carry his letters to the shores which they had visited together. Also, Epaphras was a Colossian. St Paul was encouraging them to carry on the good work of the Lord Jesus, as he also showed them all his affairs while he lived.

"All my state, my affairs the things relating to me." Tychicus, the bearer of this letter (cf. Eph.6:12). Paul at his closing in writing the Epistles to the various Churches did not hide anything from Tychicus his beloved brother and a faithful minister and fellow servant of the Lord Jesus. He opened all his own affairs to him and showed him all things concerning the kingdom. Then he said in the letter that he was giving him a letter to take to them and that he was doing so for a purpose.

"Whom I have sent unto you for the same purpose." Which was to know their state of affairs? Paul had a twofold purpose in sending Tychicus. That he might know your state, "Better," and that ye might know our state the things concerning us. This means that he was asking how was he getting on and coping with life and the church affairs while he was in prison. "Comfort your hearts." This is to give encouragement rather than consolation. Paul told his brothers in the Lord to encourage the members especially those in Colossians to strengthen themselves and be lifted up in the Lord.

"With Onesimus, a faithful and beloved brother," This is the co-bearer of the letter and Philemon the runaway slave. "Who is one of you," Now he is a brother in Christ. Paul was saying that Onesimus will be there among you all, also; he is my faithful and beloved brother and he is one of you, and he is also bringing the letter along with the other and that you should receive him although he is Philemon's runaway slave. In other words, although he was a slave, and he ran – away from Philemon his master, he was now saved and changed, and a brother to me Paul, in the Lord, so accept him as one of you.

"Aristarchus my fellow – prisoner," Aristarchus was a fellow prisoner of Paul. He was from Thessalonica and he accompanied St. Paul to Jerusalem (Acts 19:29; ch. 20:4) He was also in Rome with St. Paul, Marcus, and John Mark who was one rejected by St. Paul (Acts 15:36–39). Since they could not get along, they had some disagreements, but now they are both in agreement and he is now commended as a fellow-servant. (2 Timothy 4:11) He was also a nephew or cousin to Barnabas.

"And Jesus, which is called Justus, Joshua, a common name or ordinary name," These are of the circumcision and Jewish Christians. These followed the law and had their circumcision done after that order. Only these men who were Jewish friends of St. Paul were there for him and with him to stand beside him, and to help to hold up his hands in times of distress, with his mission to the Gentiles. There are times when Paul really needed sympathetic friends around him, but there were very few of the Jews. "A comfort," the word (Paregoric) comes from the same root word, which also means to lessen pain or to give ease. Referring to Paul's statement, he was under great pain carrying the burden of the ministry and his imprisonment and needed the comfort of his fellow – workers in the faith.

These brothers in the faith have become a great source of strength to him in his present condition. He must have given thanks to God for these few brothers who comforted him in these times of distress, even in his times of illness with the thorn in his flesh and imprisonment.

"Epaphras, who is one of you, a servant of Christ, Could it be that this brother was one of the founders or officials of the Church in Colossae? He brought St. Paul news of the condition of the state of things in the Church at Colossae. He was continually laboring fervently for the Apostle in prayer. He was a man of prayer, and when things were not going right in the church, he would pray about it and God always showed up and changed the wrong into right. He was also an intercessor and he would go to the last mile in strenuous intercession, wrestling with God like Jacob wrestled with the angel, on the Colossian behalf. "That ye may stand" If you are standing for Christ stand firm on both legs with all your strength and mature in the will of God.

"For I bear him record, that he hath a great zeal for you," This is what Paul was saying that he bore record of him Epaphras, that he has a great zeal for them and for all those that are in Laodicea and those in Hierapolis also. This then is what Paul could mean with expending painful toil to all the saints. The love and zeal of this brother had created a great bond between them all.

"Luke the beloved physician and Demas greet you". Doctor Luke was a dear and trusted friend of St. Paul and was with him for at least the first two years of his imprisonment. This can be found in the Book of Acts. (Acts 24:27) I believe that one of the reasons why Paul was very happy for the opportunity to have Doctor Luke with him was because Luke being a doctor or physician could attend to him where his physical health was concerned. "Demas" is a person who was mentioned in the book of (2 Timothy 4:10–11), that he had deserted the Apostle Paul for this present world. The information concerning Demas as mentioned here is not certain when this was written, whether before or after the second Epistle of Timothy. All we read is that Demas has forsaken Paul because he loved this present world. Some have thought that this Epistle was written after; and then it was evidence that although Demas forsook Paul, yet he did not forsook Christ; or he forsook him but for a time, and recovered himself again, and Paul did forgive him and owned him as a brother. Therefore in serving Christ and being in fellowship with the brethren, we should not have break or an interval between. In other words, we should continue on the straight path.

"Salute the brethren which are in Laodicea, and Nymphas," To my mind, it seems that the church in Laodicea had a wonderful brother with a wonderful spirit in the fellowship, his name was Nymphas. The name Nymphas in Greek means masculine or feminine. Here Nymphas in (Col. 4:15) as one lived in Colossae, and had a church in his house; that is, a religious family, where the several parts, of worship were daily performed; or some part of the congregation met there, because they had no public places of worship allowed at that time, and they were forced to assemble in private houses, because they were fearful of their enemies. You could see the value of this brother to the Laodicea, and Colossians brethren that is why he was saluted and recognized.

"And when this Epistle is read among you," or to be read in public to the church. Paul seemed to be referring to this as an epistle from Laodicea, which most likely means that this and other letters were to be circulated to all the various churches in the province of Asia. After receiving the letters from Paul the prisoner, they had to make copies by hand and pass them on to the various churches. Great effort was made to preserve the original copies; (A.T. Robertson, Word Pictures of the New Testament, 1V, p513).

"And say to Archippus, take heed to the ministry which thou hath received in the Lord," This person Archippus is mentioned in Philemon verse two in such a way as to suggest that he was a member of Philemon's household, probably his son or brother. The Colossian church was ordered to remind or admonish him to mind his work as a minister, and to take heed to fulfill it all. He had to be diligent and careful in all the parts of it and to preserve it to the end. This ministry we observed is one we received with honor, for it is received in the Lord, and is by his appointment and command. Those who received it must fulfill or do all its duties. To fail to do so means that their account on that final day will be a sad one of negligence. Hence Paul admonished them to remind Archippus to take heed of the ministry.

"The salutation by the hands of me Paul, remember my bonds," Paul adds his salutations in his handwriting. That means, he's saying to them, "Hello, remember my bonds" Think of me in my bonds; think of me in my chains; think of me in prison. The chains were probably clamped on his hand when he was writing this salutation. So he has penned this salutation and it was a direct appeal for them to pray for his release? He appealed for them to pray that his sentence would be ended and that he'd be out of prison and the chains would be off so that he would be able to feel like himself again. Now that he has finished his appeal, he pronounced on them the grace and favor of God to go with them. This meant that God's blessing with grace would be with them always. And he concluded by saying, Amen.

St. Paul was encouraged by his fellow brothers and workers in the Lord to hold the call of the Lord in high esteem or at the forefront of everything, so, as to fulfill the call of God upon their lives. Also, a brother like Onesimus who was a runaway slave, they were advised to receive him back as a brother in the Lord, because he was now changed and saved, living for Jesus. He is now one of you. Paul also used his fellow brothers to carry the Epistles to the various churches and members. For example, Epaphras was sent to Colossians because he was one of them from Colossae. So

Epaphras was told to encourage the members of the Colossians Church to strengthen themselves in the Lord.

St. Paul knowing that he could not go on the journeys to the different churches as he used to owing to his imprisonment, wrote epistles and sent them to the churches by his beloved brothers in the Lord, namely Tychicus, Onesimus, and Epaphras. As Paul opened up and related to them all of his heart's secrets about his affairs and state, his encouragement to them was that they should be fair and just in all things, and also to all the churches that they too may know what was happening to him in prison. He also told them to read the information very clearly to all the churches that they may understand.

He told Archippus to take heed to the ministry which he has from the Lord Jesus, and that he should carry it out to its fullest. He should also remember that such a call is a lifetime job, and God is expecting him to or requiring his diligence and consistency on the job. He must also remember that God does not discharge his servant and they do not retire. At the end of his salutation, he indirectly appeals to them to pray for him that the time would come soon for his release from his imprisonment with the chains.

Study Points

- Who was Onesimus?

- What was the relationship of John Mark to Barnabas?

- Which of the fellow-servant of Paul was a doctor?

- Take heed to the ministry which thou hast from the Lord Jesus that you fulfill it. To whom was Paul speaking?

- Which of Paul's fellow-servant deserted him for this present world?

HENRY

CHAPTER 9

AN OVERALL VIEW OF THE BOOK OF COLOSSIANS

As an overall view and also an extension of the book of Colossians, I have looked at the historical, cultural, and theological issues that impinge on or arise from the text. I also hit on the analogies with the present situations so as to be able to open up effectively on the epistles. This also includes learning to integrate faith and love with authority in daily Christian living.

Colossae known today as Turkey was a city church of wonderful believers founded by Epaphras although St. Paul never visited that church he always sent letters to them. As workers together with Christ sometimes we would like to visit certain of our sister churches but we can't. So, in turn, we would send messages of encouragement and up "liftmen" to them, so as to strengthen them. Paul did the very same thing. They always send gifts to Paul as a part of their history to him personally, even when he was in prison.

As a part of their culture there, as Colossians, they worshiped angels and had a great belief in evil spirits, which oftentimes coincided with the teachings of the church. So St. Paul as a wise, knowledgeable, and understanding apostle, dealt with the matter in a very commendable way which caused the Colossian church to love him more, obey him, and love the Lord Jesus Christ more. He encouraged and counseled them to be obedient to the teachings of Christ to exalt his name and to keep hoisting the name and work of Christ at all times.

Paul also developed a concrete love for the Colossians church that he called them his dearly beloved, according to the letter he sent to them at Colossae, again although in their cultural pursuit, they were plagued with the tradition of men (Mark 7:8) Elements of the world (Gal. 4:3) referring to the Jewish Ordinances, as a shadow of things to come and got them confused. Next was in line the referring to the chasing of the body in (Colossian 4:23) which seems to men an exaggerated self-humiliation like that which has been joined to ascetic practices, and has shown itself by the devoted wearing rags himself being exposed to insult and living by begging.

Another part of the cultural heritage is that they built a church in honor of the Archangel at the entrance of the chasm. A counsel was there at the neighboring town of Laodicea and Theodore speaks of it as existing in the same region. Literally, this also means indulging in fleshly abomination. When Paul heard of these faults he did not ill-speak the Colossians and discuss them with others. He prayed for them and wrote letters to them as he discussed with them and helped them to see where they were being misled, and how they could be back on the right track as children of the Most High God, who were walking in the precepts of Christ.

Paul also reminded them that they should not fear evil spirits when they were being delivered from the kingdom of darkness, and were now in the kingdom of light. Therefore they could not serve God and the devil at the same time. If they were of the enemy of their souls, they would be in darkness, and they would be stumbling. Since they were in the light, they were to walk as children of light. Certainly, this does apply to us today as we must walk as children of the light once we are named by the name of Christ and we are walking with him. Therefore, even they as well as us have to depend on the wonderful name of Jesus which is our "Strong Tower," and the righteous run into it and are saved. When the enemy rises up against us we should plead the blood of Jesus Christ against it and he will flee, because he is totally afraid of the blood of Jesus Christ, God's Son.

If things are happening to us as God's children, and we are uncomfortable about them, let's fix or place our faith on the things above where Christ sits at the right hand of the Father, (God). Literally. don't allow any man, woman, or child to turn you away from the Lord because in the long run, you will be the loser and you will be found wanting.

The Colossian church too heeded Paul's warning and counseling and they were safe afterward. That's why Paul was always very proud of them because they took his wise counseling.

Speaking of following Christ as St. Paul stated, this calls for a steadfastness that must be implied. If Ephesians can be labeled the epistle that portrays the "Church of Christ" then this is because of their devotion, steadfastness, and their love for Christ. Then the Colossians must surely be "The Christ of the Church", the book of the Ephesians focuses on the church as the "Body," but in the book of Colossians the focus is on the church as the "Head". Like Ephesians, the little book of Colossians is divided nearly in half where the first portion is doctrinal (Chapters One and Two) while the second portion is practical, (Chapters Three and Four).

Paul's purpose is to show that Christ is preeminent first and foremost in everything and in the Christian life one should reflect that priority, because believers are rooted in him, hidden in him, and completed in him. It is utterly inconsistent to live a life without him, being clothed in his love with his peace ruling in their hearts. They are equipped to make Christ in every area of their lives as head.

As the head of the church says to Paul to the Colossians in (Col. 1:18), he is the firstborn of the dead; Our Jesus was the first to be risen from the dead with a spiritual and moral body (1 Cor. 15:20) On the resurrection day Jesus became the head of the church. The New Testament Church began shortly after His resurrection when His disciples received the baptism of the Holy Spirit. The fact that Jesus was the firstborn from the dead, implies the subsequent resurrection of all those for whom he died. So indeed he is the head of the body, which is the Church, who is the beginning that in all things he might have the preeminence.

St. Paul also enlightened the Colossians that Jesus Christ is the Reconciliator of all things, (Colossian 1:19–20). This means that in him all the fullness of the God Head dwells. This statement is dealt with by St. Paul on the plainest terms. The full and complete God Head with all that it represents resides in Christ Jesus, (Heb. 1:8); (John 1:1)

It says "In the beginning was the Word, and the Word was with God and the Word was God," This then is the mystery, and only those to whom this is revealed will understand it. Jesus is very God and very man. The true humanity of Jesus is the climax of the history of creation and at the same time the commencing of the new creation.

So from eternity to time back to eternity, Jesus has been in his very nature, the image of God the Father. Therefore Jesus resembles him perfectly; he is not an imitation of him. He is the full image of him, in the character and life of God the Father. Therefore it is quite right for him to be the image of His Father. Again in (Romans 2: 4 – 20) Paul states "that those who reject Christ's offer as reconciliatory remains as God's enemy," but if they accept him and make peace with God through Jesus Christ's blood of the cross, God will accept them as his very own. This act was done in the very body of Jesus' flesh through his death on the cross, that he may present us holy, not be blamed, and not be reproached in His sight.

Now therefore taking a good look at the ongoing human response of faith that Paul stated in (Colossians 1:25) which is necessary, we as Christians must play our part in living for Christ, and do so very well too, so as to continue in the faith. We must maintain a preserving faith in him as Lord and Savior. In other words, we must be grounded and settled in the teachings of Christ that we received through the Apostles or his servants. We must not return to our former state of hopelessness with its soul-destroying vices, according to (Heb. 10:38). Mathew Henry in his commentary[6] of the 9Th Volume in chapter 1 page 7 says, "If ye continue in the faith, grounded and settled and be not moved away from the hope of the gospel, which ye have heard and which was preached to every creature that is in all creation which is under the heaven." I Paul your minister admonish you Colossians to stand fast and cherish

---

[6] Mathew Henry's Commentary of the 9th Volume in the Capture (1) of page (9) "If ye continue in the faith, grounded and settled and be not moved away from the hope."

the hope that's in you. Keep always alive in Christ and don't look back at the things that you have left in the past.

An account of the acceptance of Christ in our lives as the church, the world is waiting to see the church well-balanced. If we live dedicated and disciplined lives and do what we are supposed to do, we would bear the kind of fruit God wants us to bear, and the world would want to be like us in the long run. We also have to spend quality time with God and don't allow our lights or lamps to go out. By this, it means that the little things that are not right in the sight of God, we should not let them be involved in our lives, because it's the little foxes that spoil the grapes. These little things will hinder our progress with the Father. Therefore, we have to choose to do the right at all times and not continue to do the things that are not right. Temptation is pressure that's applied to your faith, when it comes, don't quit.

When we choose to do right, Christ assists us with his grace which gives us the strength every time to overcome the temptation. Jesus died to let us have victory over circumstances, so we have to submit to God and resist the devil and he will flee from us. This is done through prayer and the knowledge of the Word of God (James 4:7). Viewing the Church today, in my eyes, I believe we oftentimes are being found in the same positions and faults as the Colossian Christians. But we all must remember where Jesus Christ as our reconciliatory took us from and where he wants us to go with him. Then we must hold straight and fast to the profession of our faith.

At this juncture, the church here is getting very worldly, while the world is getting more like the church. I can see that there is a mixing and the church cannot mix with the world. We can't be the two at the same time. This makes it very difficult for those who really want to serve the Lord and are looking for the right example or mentors. Next, we must serve him as Lord and reverence him there and now, because of the purpose for which he came to us here on the earth. We also must realize the privilege we have, to be a part of him here when we give Him our heart in full surrender.

That means we are not our own; we belong to him because we are bought with a great price, the blood of Jesus Christ the only begotten Son of God. This also tells me that we as Christians cannot afford to live as we like, talk as we like, and go places as we like. Not because we are set free. Indeed, we are free but with accountability, meaning we have to give an account of how we handle our freedom here on earth, to God the Father on the Judgment day. Therefore we ought to be very careful how we live. Paul says; "Be careful for nothing," so even in our conversation, we should not do so idly less we say things displeasing to the Holy Spirit.

No wonder the writer realized what the loving Creator is to him as he wrote this song;

"All to Jesus I Surrender,

Humble at His feet I bow,

Worldly pleasures all forsaken;

Take me, Jesus, take me now."

Again, we are not to waste time because time wasted cannot be regained. We are to work the works of righteousness while it is day, for the night cometh when no man can work. There will come a time in all of our lives when we won't be able to do any more work, and that is why we must work hard and do it well so that we will be able to hear well done at the end of our days, for a good work done. Also, in our work as we go along, winning souls is our goal, and if we can win and carry souls with us to heaven, we will gain a beautiful crown decorated with stars according to the number of souls we have won. Then of a truth, we will have something to lay at our Master's feet as we march in the home that will be for all those who are redeemed by the blood of the Lamb.

COLOSSIANS

INSTRUCTORS GUIDE ANSWERS

Chapter ONE ANSWERS:

QUESTION (1)   Lord lay not this sin to their charge (Acts 7: 60)

QUESTION (2)   Immediately there fell from his eyes as it had been scaled, (Acts 9:18)

QUESTION (3)   I have fought a good fight, I have finished my course, (2Tim. 4:7)

QUESTION (4)   A certain disciple from Damascus named Ananias (Acts 9:17)

QUESTION (5)   He fell to the ground as a bright light shone on him from above and a Voice said "Saul, Saul, why persecutest thou me. ......I am Jesus whom thou persecutest". (Acts 9:4–5)

Chapter TWO ANSWERS

QUESTION (1)   No, (Acts 19:26) No mention in Acts.

QUESTION (2)   To keep them away from false doctrines and to stick to the truth

QUESTION (3)   Because he is the Head of that body which is the Church.

QUESTION (4)   He was in prison at Rome, (Ephesians 6:21–22)

QUESTION (5)   According to the book of Colossians the person who was acting as the minister of the Church there, was, "Epaphras"

Chapter THREE ANSWERS

QUESTION (1) Paul referred to his Apostleship because he was unknown to the Colossian Church and he was also numbered with the twelve Apostles because he had seen the risen Lord, (1 Cor. 15:8).

QUESTION (2)   St. Paul was the spiritual father of Timothy. (1 Timothy 1:2, 18)

QUESTION (3) St. Paul had never gone to the Colossians Church.

QUESTION (4) The foundation of all Christian character and conduct is to understand God's plans and purpose for our lives.

QUESTION (5) According to Colossians in the chapter, (Col. 1:11) we should be strengthened with all might, because we are engaged in a spiritual conflict and need spiritual power from God, (Ephesians 6:10, ff)

Chapter FOUR ANSWERS

QUESTION (1) For in Him dwelleth the fullness of the God Head bodily, and ye are complete in Him, which is the Head of all principality and power.

QUESTION (2) Because the Holy Spirit which is a member of the God Head, did the job.

QUESTION (3) Counselor, Mighty God, and Prince of Peace.

QUESTION (4) By reconciling God and man on the cross.

QUESTION (5)   The evidence that Jesus was not only the Son of God, but the Word "In the beginning was the Word and the Word was with God and the Word was God.

Chapter FIVE ANSWERS:-

QUESTION (1)   His main reason for endurance was that the Church at Colossae may know that it was for their sake.

QUESTION (2)   The Christian's walk as Paul would have the Colossians do it, was that they would walk the walk and talk the talk.

QUESTION (3)   Paul was warning the Colossians to be aware of the lurking enemy who would spoil and kidnap them.

QUESTION (4)   The circumcision of which St. Paul spoke about to the Colossians was the putting off of the body or flesh, or the old man, and put on Christ in the Spirit, which represents the new man.

QUESTION (5)   Paul instructed the Colossians to let their physical members be instruments of righteousness unto God and not unto unrighteousness unto sin. (Romans 6:11–14).

Chapter SIX ANSWERS:-

QUESTION (1) Explain; "Let no man beguile you…" Don't allow anyone to rob you of your prize or present from the Lord Jesus.

QUESTION (2) Death here means separation from God.

QUESTION (3) We die with Christ at conversion, as we ask Him to come into our hearts and take up residence. (Romans 6:2–4; Ch. 6:11)

QUESTION (4) We should not use symbols of Christ or instead of Christ, because since He has come, He is the real substance.

QUESTION (5) An example of one of the false philosophies that the Colossians were being warned against was the worship of angels.

Chapter SEVEN ANSWERS:-

QUESTION (1) Since the Colossians were newborn Christians, they should seek the things which are above.

QUESTION (2)   Now that they are dead to the world their lives are hidden with Christ in God.

QUESTION (3)   Three of the deeds that should be put away in the flesh are uncleanness, fornication, and covetousness.

QUESTION (4)   An example of three of the things that should be put on as dearly beloved are bowels of mercy, kindness, and meekness.

QUESTION (5)   Then above all things, the most important of all things that they should put on is charity.

Chapter EIGHT ANSWERS:-

QUESTION (1)   Onesimus was a runaway slave of Philemon.

QUESTION (2)   John Mark was the nephew of Barnabas.

QUESTION (3)   St. Paul's fellow-servant, Luke was a doctor in the company.

QUESTION (4)   Archippus was told or instructed by St. Paul to take heed to the ministry which was given to him by the Lord Jesus; and that he should fulfill it.

QUESTION (5)   Demas was one of St. Paul's fellow – brothers who deserted him for the world, or for the things of the world.

HENRY

RESOURCES

Biscoe, History of the Acts confirmed Ch.VI
Milman Dean of the Contempary on the acts,
Mr. Humphrey Contempary on the Acts
Abbott, T.K.A. Critical and Exegetical Commentary of the Epistles to the Ephesians and to the Colossians. In the International Critical Commentary, Edinburgh: T. &.T Clark, n.d.

Barnes, Albert, Notes on the New Testament Explanatory and Practical – Ephesians Philippians and Colossians. Ed, by Robert Frew. Grand Rapids Baker, 1950.

Bruce, F.F. Commentary on The Epistle to The Ephesians and the Colossians in the New International Commentary on the New Testament: Grand Rapids Eerdmans, 1957.

Calvin John Commentary on the Epistle to the Philippians, Colossians, and Thessalonians. Trans and, ed, and edly John Pringle, Grand; Eerdmans 1948.

Abbott T.K. A. Critical and Exegetical Commentary of the Epistles to the Ephesians and the Colossians, In the International Critical Commentary, Edinburgh T & T Clark n.d.

Barns Albert, Notes on the New Testament, Explanatory and Practical – Ephesians

Philippians and Colossians ED. by Robert Frew Grand Rapids Baker 1950.

Bruce F.F. Commentary on the Epistles to the Ephesians and the Colossians. In the New International Commentary on the New Testament Grand Rapids Erdmands 1957.

Moule, H.C.G. The Epistle of Paul the Apostle to the Colossians and Philemon, In the Cambridge Bible for School and College. Cambridge University Press reprinted 1932.

Bruce F.F. Commentary on the Epistle to the Ephesians and the Colossians. In the New International Commentary on the New Testament, Grand Rapids Erdmands 1959.

Hendrikson, Williams, Exposition of Colossians and Philemon. New Testament Commentary Grand Rapids, Baker, 1964.

Ironside, Harry, A Lectures on the Epistle to the Colossians Neptune; N. J. Loizeaux Brothers 1955.
Harrison Evett, F. Colossians, Christ All Sufficient, Chicago: Moody Press, 1971.

Nicholson, William R. Popular Studies in Colossians Ed. by James M. Gray. Grand Rapids Kregel, n.d.

Peake, A.S. The Epistle to the Colossians. In the

Expositor's Greek New Testament, Grand Rapids, Eerdmans, n.d.

Thomas W.H. Griffith Christ Pro – Eminent Studies in the Epistle to the Colossians, Chicago: Moody Press,1923.

Thomas, W. H. Griffith, Christ Pre – Eminent Studies in the Epistle to the Colossians, Chicago: Moody, Press. 1923.

Wuest, Kenneth S. Ephesians and Colossians. In The Greek New Testament for the English Reader; Grand Rapids: Eerdamns 1953.

Peake, A. S. The Epistle to the Colossians. In the Expositors Greek New Testament Grand Rapids: Eerdmans n.d.
Falwell, Jerry, D. D. D. Litt. Liberty Bible Commentary of the New Testament

Hindson, Edwards E. III Koll Woodrow Michael IV Liberty University. B.S. 491, 2, 153, (982) I.S.B.N. 0 – 8407 – 5257 – (set)

McDonald, H. D. Commentary on Colossians and to Philemon, Waco: Word Books 1980.

Mathew Henry's Commentary on the New Testament with preface by Spurgeon C.H

Volume 9. Colossians to James, Bakes Book House, Grand Rapids Michigan (49506)

Made in the USA
Middletown, DE
21 July 2024

57445784R00068